THE
Path of Life

Warren Ravenscroft

The Path of Life
© Warren Ravenscroft 2024

Paperback ISBN: 978-0-6486422-8-2
eBook ISBN: 978-0-6486422-5-1

Scripture taken from the New King James Version®.
Copyright © 1982 by Thomas Nelson.
Used by permission. All rights reserved.

All rights reserved. No part of this publication may be reproduced, stored in a retrieval system, or transmitted in any form or by any means electronic, mechanical, photocopying, recording, or therwise, without the prior written permission of the author.

Published in Australia by Warren Ravenscroft
www.wittonbooks.com

 A catalogue record for this book is available from the National Library of Australia

"You will show me the path of life;
In Your presence is fullness of joy;
At Your right hand
are pleasures forevermore."

Psalm 16:11

Contents

PART 1   7

Foreword   9

Promise One: A Great Nation 13
    Called to Lead 15
    The Second Forty Years 25
    The Third Forty Years 37
    A Prayer of Moses 91

Promise Two: A Land of Their Own 95
    The Soldier of the Lord 97

Promise Three: A Blessing to Others 119
    Others Blessed 121

PART 2   125

Further Insights 127
   The Journey 129
   The Passover 137
   Water Supplied 145
   The Tabernacle 151
   The Camp of Israel 171
   Midianites 175
   Jericho and Beyond 183
   The Southern Conquest 191

Foreshadows of Jesus 195
The Path of Life 219
A Benediction 239

CHARTS

Ancestry: Moses 12
The Ten Plagues of Egypt 41
Ancestry: Joshua 96
The Camp of Israel 172
Ancestry: Jesus 190
Similarities Between the Passover and Jesus 198
Tabernacle, Feast and *I AM*s 210
Similarities Between Moses and Jesus 215
Joshua, a Foreshadowing of Jesus 217

Other books by the Author 243

Foreword

When reading the Bible and the events, parables and stories, the reader can often be left in awe or wonder at how God dealt with people and situations. A verse which explains what we may not understand or comprehend says,

> "For My thoughts are not your thoughts,
> nor are your ways My ways," says the Lord.
> "For as the heavens are higher than the earth,
> so are My ways higher than your ways,
> and My thoughts than your thoughts."
>
> Isaiah 55:8–9

While Paul, when writing his first letter to the Corinthians encouraged them to obtain the mind of Christ (1 Corinthians 2:16), we will never be able to fathom Father God and His ordained will for each of our lives.

Only through obedience to the revealed will of God as He reveals Himself to your own heart, by exercising faith and trust, can we please the One who called us to be His own.

While He calls us to walk unfamiliar paths and directs each step we take, we must trust Father God to know best despite the circumstances we may find ourselves in.

If the Father has brought us to it, then He will bring us through whatever He chose for us to complete in His own time. Our part is to always remain faithful, as we draw closer to Him in our relationship, knowing He won't permit anything to come to us that we are incapable of overcoming with the Holy Spirit's direction and guidance.

The Old Testament patriarchs and prophets, followed the directions personally given to them by Father God. They were obedient to His will, although hard times, disrespect, loneliness and much more accompanied their journey.

Moses was called by God to lead His people out of captivity, but long before Moses was compelled to carry out in obedience what God had ordained, God had structured and guided his life to fulfil His plan and purpose. Although Moses made excuses as to his suitability, Father God had crossed every 'T' and dotted every 'I' so that he was the right person at the right time.

Joshua was also called to follow the lead of Moses, as he proved faithful in all things when sent out as a spy and his dealing with the children of Israel. He had a deep sense of loyalty not only to God but to those who followed him and accepted his leadership.

Foreword

Just like Moses and Joshua, as we acknowledge the plan Father God has for each of us, through patience, persistence, perseverance, and obedience, we will be found as true shepherds, ministering to those of God's choosing.

Did the children of Israel ever reach and live as Father God ordained, or did they settle for something else by their choosing? While Moses led the people God had called to Himself, and Joshua did his best to guide the wayward chosen to understand and accept the ways of God, did they ever find the true promised land and the three promises to Abraham fulfilled?

Only by obedience and acceptance of God's will for each person, those whom Father God has chosen, will find the real promised land and eternal joy that accompanies complete adherence to what the Father has ordained.

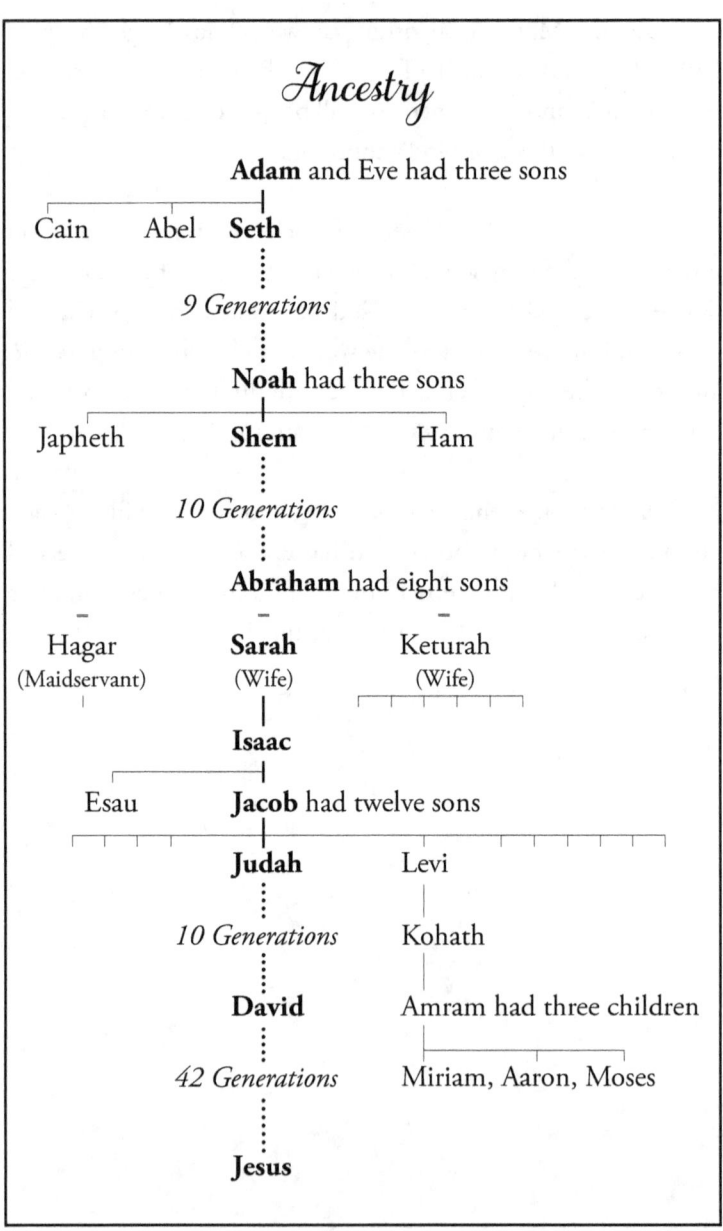

Promise One:

A GREAT NATION

Called to Lead: The First Forty Years

To understand the calling of Moses, we need to search the past generations and what Father God ordained to bring about. God called Abram, along with his family, to go to a place He would show him. Because Abram obeyed the known will of God, He gave him three promises. Abram who would become Abraham was chosen to be one of the forefathers whom the Israelites would identify with. The other two would be Isaac and Jacob, who also had his name changed to Israel.

God outlined His promises to Abram covenanting with him to:

- Give him a land of his own.
- His descendants would be a mighty nation.
- His descendants would be a blessing throughout the earth.

Genesis 17:4–9

About three hundred and fifty years would pass before Joseph, a Hebrew, second in command to Pharaoh, could settle his father Jacob and his families into the land of Goshen, in the land of Egypt. Over the next three hundred years, the Hebrews would grow in number until the Pharaoh of the day saw them as a threat to his reign.

A question to be asked is, "Who were the Egyptians and where did they come from?" As we look at ancestry, they were originally descended from one of Noah's sons called Ham. He had a son called Canaan who sinned in the sight of the Lord. While Noah blessed his other two sons, Japheth and Shem, Ham and all his descendants were cursed.

Pharaoh was unaware of Joseph and what he had done for the Egyptians and his predecessors. Many families, from the then-known area, had moved to Egypt including Jacob and his family during the severe famine. What this Pharaoh did notice was that those who were the inhabitants of Goshen were growing in numbers to the point that Pharaoh showed his concern that if war broke out, these people might fight against the Egyptians. Instead of allying with these Hebrews, Pharaoh increased their workload.

Pharaoh noticed the more he oppressed the Hebrew people, the more they grew in numbers. He told the Hebrew midwives to kill the male babies when they were born, but because they feared God, they disobeyed the Pharaoh's orders. Pharaoh was not pleased with their response to his command so he ordered all newborn boy babies to be thrown into the river.

The First Forty Years

The Egyptians worshipped three gods associated with the Nile River. They were Khnum, the guardian of the river's source, Hapi, the spirit of the Nile, and Osiris, the Nile's bloodstream. Hapi was worshipped by casting offerings annually into the river's rising water. Unlike the worship of Baal, none of the Nile's gods required human sacrifice.

A family from the tribe of Levi, Amram the father, Jochebed the mother, Miriam the daughter and Aaron a son lived in Goshen. When the parents became aware that Jochebed was with child, they knew of Pharaoh's decree. When the baby boy was born, he was of beautiful appearance. The Egyptians would have destroyed him, but Jochebed hid their baby for three months. When it was no longer feasible for his birth to be concealed, Jochebed took a woven basket, lined it with pitch, placed the baby inside, and then concealed the baby and basket amongst the bull-rushes. Miriam, the older daughter, was left to observe the baby's safety.

During the day, the daughter of Pharaoh, along with her attendants, came to wash. When the basket was noticed, she gave an order for it to be brought to her. When the basket was opened, the baby inside cried. The heart of Pharaoh's daughter was full of compassion for this little helpless life. It is believed that each of the maidservants offered herself to the baby for milk, but each was rejected. As Miriam observed what had transpired, she offered to find a suitable wet nurse for the baby. When Jochebed offered herself to the baby, she was instantly accepted, but this is not recorded in the Bible so is unsubstantiated.

It is unclear what happened between the daughter of Pharaoh and the Hebrew mother, Jochebed. The account in Exodus records the following:

> *Then the Pharaoh's daughter said to her,*
> *"Take this child away and nurse him for me,*
> *and I will give you your wages."*
> *So the woman took the child and nursed him.*
> *And the child grew,*
> *and she brought him to Pharaoh's daughter,*
> *and he became her son.*
>
> Exodus 2:9–10

Luke, many years later, wrote about Moses and what transpired between the daughter of Pharaoh and Jochebed.

> *"But when he was set out,*
> *Pharaoh's daughter took him away*
> *and brought him up as her own son."*
>
> Acts 7:21

One suggests that the mother took him back to their home before taking him to the palace, possibly between the age of three and five as this was the weaning time for a child. Another scenario is that Jochebed went to the palace and served as a nursemaid until the child was weaned, and was paid to look after the child.

If the child, whom the daughter of Pharaoh called Moses, because she drew him out of the water, had stayed with Jochebed in their home for the duration, this would have given her ample time to instruct Moses in the ways of the Hebrews, including teaching him both languages, Hebrew and Egyptian. One would imagine that Hebrews were multilingual as they would have been required to understand the commands of their taskmasters and comply with their orders.

Luke when writing his account from the Old Testament scriptures, and maybe oral tradition, could have meant that when the child had been weaned (set out), Pharaoh's daughter took him away to be trained as her son. The details of what happened are obscured. What we do know is what's recorded in the Book of Proverbs, for it says,

"Train up a child when they are young,
and when they are old they will not depart from it."

Proverbs 22:6

Pharaoh's daughter was true to her word and trained Moses in all the ways of the Egyptians, as he became mighty in words and deeds, or otherwise, well educated. Pharaoh's daughter would have adorned Moses in the best of Egyptian clothes, and have been taught about the numerous gods of the Egyptians and how they were observed and worshipped. He would have recognised that Pharaoh regarded himself as the supreme god, and was to be obeyed without question, as to disobey the known will of Pharaoh, could be certain death.

Moses was in all ways taught and trained in Egyptian life and all the pleasures that accompanied his lifestyle. But one unclear thing is how Moses, being a Hebrew was accepted in the palace. His ancestor was Joseph, and also a Hebrew. How was the Egyptian Moses accepted when in Joseph's time they were seen as an abomination and would not even eat with the Hebrews? Was Moses ever subjected to the same type of treatment, but under the shadow of the daughter of Pharaoh, was the exception? We are not told.

How long Moses knew he was of Hebrew descent is unclear, but the day came when he chose to remove himself from all things Egyptian, for it is recorded,

"By faith Moses, when he became of age,

refused to be called the son of Pharaoh's daughter,

choosing rather to suffer affliction with the people of God

than to enjoy the passing pleasures of sin."

Hebrews 11:24–25

Moses had openly identified himself as a Hebrew and stood with Israel and the chosen children of God. The question to be asked is, "Why, after forty years, did Moses suddenly have a complete change in the life he lived?" A second question is,

"What prompted this course of action?" A possible answer could have been written by Luke, the writer of the New Testament book, 'The Acts of the Apostles' so many years later when he recorded the following.

> *"And Moses was learned in all the wisdom of the Egyptians, and was mighty in words and deeds."*
>
> Acts 7:22

A possible scenario could answer both of the previous questions. Moses would have been taught by the best teachers about the gods of Egypt and what they represented with their culture. Customs and procedures would be meticulously outlined to the smallest detail as to how he should present himself and act at all times, especially in the presence of Pharaoh who demanded complete respect, as he saw himself as the supreme god.

Ancient history may have been taught, as to their ancestors and how the Egyptians became a nation to be reckoned with. Maybe at one session, he read that a Hebrew slave rose to power because he had insight and knowledge that those in Egypt did not have. As Moses continued to read, as his inquiring mind searched for answers, he knew that the association with Hebrews was an abomination to all Egyptians. Genesis 43:32

As Moses continued his research about the Hebrew people who were distant ancestors of his, he found the Egyptians descended from Noah and his son Ham, whereas the Hebrews had descended from Shem, another of Noah's sons. The more he read, the more he was drawn to these people, but why? Moses was about to suffer an identity crisis.

One could imagine him going to the daughter of Pharaoh and asking her about his past. Was he her child or was he adopted? The Pharaoh's daughter always knew this day would come and told Moses how she had saved his life and taken him to herself. When the truth was revealed, Moses refused to be called her son, but rather identified with the Hebrews. His life changed forever, as he restructured his life in the palace.

When Moses turned forty, he was prompted to visit these Hebrew people which he thought would add understanding to his thinking and processing, as he had identified as being of Hebrew descent. We read the following recorded by Luke.

> *"Now when he was forty years old,*
> *it came into his heart to visit his brethren,*
> *the children of Israel."*

Acts 7:23

A further revelation came to Moses when he understood in his thoughts, that he was the destined leader to free the Hebrews from slavery to the Egyptians, as the shoe was now on the other foot. The following verse can clarify this:

> *"For he supposed that his brethren would have understood that God would deliver them by his hand, but they did not understand."*
>
> Acts 7:25

Even with the best of intentions, things don't always go to plan. As Moses looked and watched the Hebrews who were working under their masters, he noticed one of the Hebrews suffered at the hands of an Egyptian. Moses chose to avenge the one who was oppressed, and when he had looked this way and that, he killed the Egyptian and buried his body in the sand. Exodus 2:12, Acts 7:24

The next day, Moses again went out to the people whom he had identified with and claimed to be one with them. As he walked and watched, Moses noticed two Hebrews fighting. He immediately went and tried to reconcile them, saying, *"Men, you are brethren; why do you wrong one another?"* Exodus 2:13, Acts 7:26

Moses had assumed that now he had revealed himself, and identified with the Hebrews, they would respect and follow his lead, but he could not have foreseen the response that was given to him. The one who was the strongest of the two, replied to Moses and pushed him away, saying, *"Who made you a ruler and judge over us?"* The Hebrew continued, *"Do you want to kill me as you did the Egyptian yesterday?"* Exodus 2:14, Acts 7:27–28

Moses realised his efforts and plans were rejected by the Hebrews, as they had no insight into the mind of Moses and how Father God had revealed secret things to him. Moses feared and said, *"Surely this thing is known!"* His future as leader of the Hebrews lay at his feet as a shattered mess. He reasoned within himself that if this was openly known, then Pharaoh would know and he would face the death penalty. So, Moses packed up and fled.

The Second Forty Years

Self-preservation was in the thoughts of Moses. He had burnt many bridges in the palace as he refused to be known as the son of Pharaoh's daughter. This fact about Moses was not recorded in the book of Exodus, but was recalled by the writer to the Hebrews when he wrote:

> *"By faith Moses, when he became of age,*
> *refused to be called the son of Pharaoh's daughter,*
> *choosing rather to suffer affliction with the people of God*
> *than to enjoy the passing pleasures of sin."*
>
> Hebrews 11:24–25

One would imagine that Moses had no idea what the future held for him, he just needed to be at least three days away from the jurisdiction of Pharaoh. Moses had a choice of at least three ways to travel. They were the three trade routes of the day and would provide food and shelter for him in his hurried venture. He could travel the 'Way of the Philistines' to Gaza, or a second option was the 'Way of Shur' to Beersheba. A third route was from 'Egypt to Arabia' to Ezion Gerber, and as Moses ended up in Midian, this was the most likely road he would have used.

The approximate distance from Egypt to Midian is about 300 miles. If Moses walked 3 miles per hour every day, for 16 hours a day, this would take about six to seven days. One could imagine that Moses hurried for the first few days until he knew he was well away from Pharaoh, then slowed down to a reasonable pace for the rest of the journey. Where he was going and where he would end up was of no concern to Moses. While he chose his way, Father God was directing his steps.

After Moses had crossed into the area of Midian, he noticed a well and sat down. He had no idea that this action would change his life and destiny forever. Because Moses was well educated, he was aware that the land of Midian was part of his ancestral heritage as was Egypt. The descendants of Midian came from Shem, one of the blessed sons of Noah. After ten generations had passed, Abraham through his second wife Keturah had six sons, one of whom was called Midian.

Six generations had passed and Moses found himself in the land of his ancestors. As he rested, he saw seven shepherdesses lead some sheep, draw water and filled the water troughs for their thirsty sheep. Before they could water their sheep, other shepherds arrived and drove them away, so they could use the water the women had drawn for their sheep. Moses showed compassion and intervened on behalf of the shepherdesses, stood up to the shepherds then helped the shepherdesses water their flock.

As the previous accounts have been written, a question needs to be asked, "Was Moses a peaceful man who did not like violence?" As I read the account of Moses and the altercation with the Egyptian overseer, did he take revenge for his fellow Hebrew or was it straight out of anger? He saw himself as the saviour of this race, and maybe the death was accidental, but then he did look this way and that.

The next day, when confronted by the two Hebrews fighting, did he again intervene out of concern and wanted to bring a peaceful resolution to the one who was hurt by his fellow man? This was not accepted by the Hebrews but met with retaliation, as Moses was falsely accused and judged for his intervention. Were Moses' actions misunderstood?

Now we have a third recorded incident about Moses and how he dealt with people. He took on the shepherds when they bullied the shepherdesses, as he provided help in their time of need. In all three accounts, Moses is observed as the one who had a sense or an awareness of injustice and in his way administered retribution for the ones involved.

Moses did not go with the shepherdesses but bid them farewell. It would appear from the Bible account, that it was only after Reuel their father, also called Jethro, Moses was asked to eat with them all. The seven daughters of Jethro, who was also the priest of Midian, told their father about the Egyptian who had helped them at the water troughs when they were harassed by the shepherds. While Moses had the heart of a Hebrew, he had the appearance of an Egyptian.

Their hospitality was offered to Moses who found himself content to live with this family. Eventually, Moses married Zipporah, one of Jethro's daughters, as he had settled into the life of a shepherd. This appealed to the deeper sense within Moses as he daily cared for the sheep. A shepherd was a full-time commitment, as he cared for the sheep's needs, all day every day, as he located places for the sheep to eat and drink that were in his care.

Moses and his wife Zipporah were blessed with a son whom Moses called Gershom. Names had meaning and often reflected the parent's past, and this name was from a Hebrew root meaning 'driven or thrust out'. Moses chose the name because he found himself a stranger in a foreign land. Exodus 2:22b

Moses would live a life of obscurity for the next forty years, as he moved around the surrounding areas. The information he gathered would prove invaluable to him in the future as God was teaching him to observe what He continued to show him. Life was so different to the previous forty years of palace life. As a contented shepherd, he was living the dream.

The gods he worshipped were a mixed bunch. There was possibly the early teaching from Jochebed, his Hebrew mother, about the One True God with mixed gods of the Egyptians, then in-depth teaching followed by the Egyptians and their gods. Now he embraced more teaching from his father-in-law the Midian priest and their acceptance of many gods and Baal worship, but this was all about to change. Nearly forty years had passed, and Moses found himself in the back end of the desert with his sheep. His life was about to take on a new direction, again.

We read the following account of Moses' travels.

> *"Now Moses was tending the flock of Jethro*
> *his father-in-law, the priest of Midian.*
> *And he led the flock to the back of the desert,*
> *and came to Horeb,*
> *the mountain of God."*
>
> Exodus 3:1

Moses was well acquainted with strange things that occurred in desert places. As he led his sheep, he noticed a burning bush. This happened in the desert when a bush would suddenly combust from the heat and burn, but what Moses saw was different. As Moses watched, the bush just burned but was not consumed. He had never witnessed anything like this before so, as his curiosity overwhelmed him, he went to witness this great phenomenon.

As Moses, with his shepherd's rod neared the unconsumed burning bush, the Angel of the Lord spoke to him.

"Moses, Moses!"
And he said, "Here I am."
Then He said, "Do not draw near this place.

> *Take your sandals off your feet,*
> *for the place you are standing is Holy Ground.*
> *I am the God of your father*
> *the God of Abraham, the God of Isaac,*
> *and the God of Jacob."*
> *And Moses hid his face,*
> *for he was afraid to look upon God.*
>
> Exodus 3:4b–6

Moses was experiencing a real-life encounter with the God of his ancestors. Whatever his past had taught him, one thing he remembered was that he could not look upon God and hid his face. At eighty years of age, God was about to call Moses to the leadership role he previously thought was his calling, but had at that time, turned sour. Moses' timing and God's timing were on different schedules. Moses is now confronted with what Father God had ordained would take place.

At 80 years of age, God is about to outline to Moses His plan for the children of Israel's deliverance. A man who was afraid to look upon God is unafraid to speak or reply to His requests. Father God outlines what He required Moses to complete because He had heard the cry of His chosen people, and it was time to deliver them from their oppressors. Father God told Moses He was giving them the lands which were presently occupied by the Canaanites, Hittites, Amorites, Perizzites,

Hivites and the Jebusites. As Moses listened, did he realise they were all descendants of the cursed son of Ham, Canaan?

The Angel of the Lord told Moses he was to go to Pharaoh. This would have been the last place Moses would want to go, as this would be like casting himself back into the fire. What was the Angel thinking? Did He not remember his past? So, Moses replied, "I am not fit to go." (Exodus 3:11). The Angel assured Moses that He would go with him and bring them all back to serve God on this mountain. Exodus 3:12

Moses remembered his last encounter with the two Hebrews and how they refused to accept his leadership when they said, *"Who made you a ruler and a judge over us?"* (Exodus 2:14a, Acts 7:27b). So, Moses asked the question as to his authority to answer their question. The Angel was ready for Moses and said:

"I AM WHO I AM."

"Thus you shall say to the children of Israel,

'I AM has sent me to you'."

Exodus 3:14

The Angel then instructed Moses to gather the elders of Israel together and to outline what God had purposed for their release from oppression. How Father God had preordained what would happen and how the Egyptians would react. How the lands of Ham's descendants, the land now flowing with milk and honey, would be their inheritance, as God had promised their forefathers. Exodus 3:15–22

Moses was antagonistic to the Angel and suggested they would not believe him. This is now the second excuse Moses offered to the Angel. As with all things, when God has made known His will, obedience is the only answer, not excuses. The Angel of the Lord told Moses to throw the rod he was holding to the ground which immediately turned into a serpent. Moses ran from it in fear, but the Angel told Moses to take it by the tail. Guess Moses had to exercise faith and trust, as he took hold of the tail, and watched as the serpent became a rod again.

But the Angel wasn't done with Moses. He told Moses to put his hand inside his clothes and then to take it out. As Moses completed the first part, his hand was leprous, like snow. He was told to repeat the procedure, and to his amazement, his hand returned to normal. Moses was then instructed to use both these signs if the elders did not believe, and if both failed, then he was to take water from the river Nile and pour it onto the dry ground and it would become blood. Did Moses remember what he had been taught about the Egyptian gods of the river Nile, Khnum, Hapi and Osiris?

As he had failed twice by providing unacceptable excuses, he tried a third, that of eloquence, in other words, he was unfit to speak to Pharaoh. This appeared to be a contradiction with what was recorded about him when he was schooled in the Egyptian palace.

> *"And Moses was learned in all the wisdom of the Egyptians, and was mighty in words and deeds."*
>
> Acts 7:22

This third excuse didn't hold water, as the Angel reminded Moses:

> *"Who has made man's mouth?*
> *Or who makes the mute, the deaf,*
> *the seeing, or the blind?*
> *Have not I, the Lord."*
>
> Exodus 4:11

Moses now revealed his real self by saying, "Send someone else" (Exodus 4:13). This was not what the Angel of the Lord required of Moses because the anger of the Lord was kindled against Moses. The Angel of the Lord reminded Moses that Aaron was a Levite and would accompany him and speak for him wherever and whenever it was necessary. To prove this to Moses, Aaron had been prompted to travel from Egypt and meet Moses. The Angel told him that when he met with his brother Aaron it would be one of joy, that he was to tell him all that had happened and been told to him in his encounter at the burning unconsumed bush. Moses made no more excuses but accepted the will of God.

As Moses was now in agreement with the Lord, He gave Moses more information about the final outcome he would have with Pharaoh. The Lord said:

> *"Then you shall say to Pharaoh,*
> *'Thus says the Lord:*
> *Israel is My son, My firstborn.*
> *So I say to you,*
> *let My son go that he may serve Me.*
> *But if you refuse to let him go,*
> *indeed I will kill your son, your firstborn'."*
>
> Exodus 4:22–23

As Moses knew the beginning and the ending, he had no idea what was contained within the in-between.

One thing remained for Moses to complete before his ordained task could take place. Moses was required to ask permission from his father-in-law, Jethro to leave. He had been a part of the family for forty years. It appeared that Moses did not outline to the priest Jethro all that had been revealed to him, but simply said:

> *"Please let me go and return*
> *to my brethren who are in Egypt,*
> *and whether they are still alive."*

And Jethro said to Moses,
"Go in peace."

Exodus 4:18

There is a quote that says, "If God brings you into any situation, trust Him to bring you through it." Paul when writing to the Romans said the quote this way.

"And we know that all things work
together for good to those
who love God, to those who are
the called according to His purpose."

Romans 8:28

Try as he may, the excuses made by Moses were not acceptable to Father God when His revealed will was made known. Only obedience to the known will of God as He reveals Himself to your own heart, is acceptable.

Moses made 4 excuses.

- Personal unfitness.   Exodus 3:11
- Fears unbelief of the people.   Exodus 4:1
- Lack of Eloquence.   Exodus 4:10
- Requests some other leader to be sent.   Exodus 4:13

God made 4 Promises of aid.

- His Divine presence.   Exodus 3:12
- Given Divine authority.   Exodus 3:3, 14
- Promised Divine Empowerment.   Exodus 4:2–8
- Promised human cooperation.   Exodus 4:14–16

Two chapters in the life of Moses had been revealed to him. Had he ever imagined what had taken place would have happened? As the third chapter opens, only faith and trust in the God who called him to His divine task will see him victorious in completing the plan of God for Moses and His chosen people.

The Third Forty Years

Moses left the comforts of Jethro's home and travelled with his family, back to Egypt.

> *"Moses took his wife and his sons*
> *and set them on a donkey,*
> *and he returned to the land of Egypt.*
> *And Moses took the rod of God in his hand."*
>
> Exodus 4:20

The Lord gave Moses specific instructions to be told to and carried out in the presence of Pharaoh. This was a test of obedience for Moses which would proceed his whole journey with the chosen people of God. As a leader, he was to lead by example, as he showed that complete obedience to the revealed will of God to them was the only acceptable answer.

During his journey back to Egypt, Moses would meet Aaron his older brother whom he had not seen for over forty years. In such a vast country from Egypt to Midian, for two people to meet at the same place could only happen under the direct guidance and control of Father God. When Moses reached the encampment, he was unexpectedly threatened with death as he had not circumcised his son, so Zipporah his wife attended to the requirement and the family once more proceeded on their ordained way.

Aaron was a Levite of the priestly tribe and was aware of the presence of God. When God told Aaron to go into the wilderness to meet his younger brother, what better place than the Mountain of God, or Mt. Horeb also known as Mt. Sinai. What a joyful meeting for them both and for Aaron to meet his brother's family. One could only imagine the excitement that filled Aaron as Moses outlined God's redemption plan for Israel and the accompanying signs. Together they travelled the distance to meet with the elders of the children of Israel. Exodus 4:27–28

As the elders accepted all that Aaron shared with them about Moses and the signs, the time was right to confront Pharaoh with their request. Moses was expecting a negative response as the Lord had told him He would harden Pharaoh's heart. Moses was not disappointed, as Pharaoh, who did not recognise God but saw himself as the supreme god, increased the hardship on the children of Israel, for we read,

> *"Let the Lord look on you (Moses) and judge,*
> *because you have made us abhorrent*
> *in the sight of Pharaoh*

> *and in the sight of his servants,*
> *to put a sword in their hand to kill us."*
>
> Exodus 5:21

The request Moses made of Pharaoh was reasonable but came with a hard-handed response. So, what had Moses asked Pharaoh to allow?

> *"Thus says the Lord God of Israel:*
> *'Let My people go,*
> *that they may hold a feast to Me in the wilderness.'*
> *The God of the Hebrews has met with us.*
> *Please, let us go three days' journey into the desert*
> *and sacrifice to the Lord our God,*
> *lest He fall upon us with pestilence or with sword."*
>
> Exodus 5:1, 3

Animal sacrifice was not acceptable in the eyes of the Egyptians, as at least four of the gods they worshipped, Ptah, Mnevis, Hathor and Amon were all associated with bulls and cows. If what the Hebrews did was witnessed by the Egyptians, they would have seen the sacrifice as an abomination directly against their deities.

Because Pharaoh had reacted so violently to the request, the Lord said to Moses,

> *"Now you will see what I shall do to Pharaoh.*
> *For with a strong hand he will let them go,*
> *and with a strong hand*
> *he will drive them out of his land."*
>
> Exodus 6:1

Moses is eighty years old and Aaron is eighty-three when they confronted Pharaoh. While it is recorded that those who sought to kill Moses were dead (Exodus 4:19), Moses asked Jethro his father-in-law to let him return to Egypt to see if his brethren were still alive (Exodus 4:18). If this included his father Amram, his mother Jochebed, Miriam his older sister and Aaron his older brother, did this also include the daughter of Pharaoh who was his adopted mother? Was she aware of Moses' return to Pharaoh's palace and his requests? We are not told as the only names recorded are Miriam and Aaron.

As God had hardened Pharaoh's heart, the next ten to twelve months would certainly test this man who thought he was god implementing his right over the One true God. Moses and Aaron went to Pharaoh a second time, where Pharaoh required a miracle of them. Aaron, not Moses, cast his rod down and it became a serpent. Pharaoh called his wise men, sorcerers and magicians who used their enchantments to counteract Aaron's serpent, but the miracle came as each rod was eaten up by the rod of Aaron, but a defeated Pharaoh did not heed them. They had won the first round, but unbeknown to Pharaoh, there were ten more to follow.

	Plague	The Egyptian god	Notes
1.	Water Turned to Blood. Exodus 7:14–25	Khnum. Guardian of river's source. Hapi. Spirit of the Nile. Osiris. Nile was his bloodstream.	Duplicated by the Egyptians. Occurred in Goshen where the Hebrews live. Dead fish. Putrid smell.
2.	Frogs. Exodus 8:1–15	Hapi. Frog goddess to Egypt. Heqt. Both related to fertility.	Duplicated by the Egyptians. Occurred in Goshen where the Hebrews live.
3.	Lice. Exodus 8:16–19	Seb. The earth god of Egypt.	Not duplicated by Egyptians. Occurred in Goshen where the Hebrews live.
4.	Flies. Exodus 8:20–32	Uatchit. The fly god of Egypt.	Hebrews not affected by any more plagues.
5.	Disease of Cattle. Exodus 9:1–7	Ptah. Mnevis. Hathor. Amon. Egyptian gods associated with bulls and cows.	Affects Egyptian Property. Death of livestock.
6.	Boils. Exodus 9:8–12	Sekhmet. Egyptian goddess of diseases. Serapis. Imhotep. Egyptian gods of healing.	Affects physical bodies. Pharaoh's magicians unable to appear.
7.	Hail. Exodus 9:13–35	Nut. Egyptian sky goddess. Isis. Seth. Egyptian agriculture deities. Shu. Egyptian god of the atmosphere.	Historical unique storm in Egypt. Pharaoh confesses his sin but later changes his mind.
8.	Locusts. Exodus 10:1–20	Serapia. Egyptian deity protector from locusts.	Pharaoh offers a compromise. Rejected.
9.	Darkness. Exodus 10:21–29	Re. Amon-re. Aten. Atum. Horus. Egyptian Sun gods. Thoth. Egyptian moon god.	Dark in Egypt at midday. Hebrews not affected. Still had light.
10.	Death of Firstborn. Exodus 12:29–36	This was a judgement of all Egypt's gods, including Pharaoh as he saw himself as the supreme god.	Pharaoh's son, his heir died. Their god in line is dead.

What God was about to do through Moses, attacked many of the gods of the Egyptians. The ten plagues would be an attack and defeat of at least twenty-five of the worshipped Egyptian gods. It should be noted that the first three plagues occurred in Goshen and the Hebrews as well as in Egypt and the Egyptians. Only the first two plagues were duplicated by the Egyptians, which showed the supremacy of God as He continued to show His strength over the gods of Egypt.

The first plague was turning the **River Nile into Blood** (Exodus 7:14–25). Three Egyptian gods were defeated. They were Khnum, the guardian of the Nile's source, Hapi, which was the spirit of the Nile, and Osiris represented the Nile's bloodstream. Both the Hebrews and the Egyptians suffered from this plague as the fish all died and the smell was putrid. The Egyptians also duplicated this plague.

The second plague was **Frogs** (Exodus 8:1–15). Hapi is again defeated as she was the Frog goddess of Egypt. Heqt is also associated with Hapi as both are related to fertility. The Hebrews also contended with the frog plague as the Egyptians were also able to duplicate the plague of frogs.

The third plague of **Lice** was the turning point for the Egyptians as they lost this battle (Exodus 8:16–19), as they could not duplicate this plague. The Egyptian god Seb represented the earth god of Egypt. The lice plague also cause grief in Goshen and the Hebrews.

The fourth plague was that of **Flies** which attacked the Egyptian god Uatchit (Exodus 8:20–32). While the plagues continued in Egypt, the Hebrews were exempt from all that was to follow.

The fifth plague was the **Disease of Cattle** (Exodus 9:1–7) and was aimed at four Egyptian gods, Ptah, Mnevis, Hathor and Amon. These gods were associated with bulls and cows, which affected Egyptian property and the death of livestock. None of the Hebrew's livestock suffered or died.

The sixth plague was that of **Boils** (Exodus 9:8–12). This plague attacked and defeated three of the gods worshipped by the Egyptians. First, there was Sekhmet, the Egyptian goddess of diseases followed by Serapis and Imhotep, the Egyptian gods of healing. Again, the effects of this plague were not inflicted on the Hebrews.

The seventh plague was that of **Hail** (Exodus 9:13–35). This occurrence attacked four of the Egyptian gods, Nut, the Egyptian sky goddess, Isis and Seth, the Egyptian agriculture deities as well as Shu, the Egyptian god of the atmosphere. The hail storm was a unique storm to occur in Egypt. While Pharaoh confessed some form of defeat, he later relinquished his fault which caused the plagues to continue.

The eighth plague was that of **Locusts** (Exodus 10:1–20). The Egyptian god Serapia was the target as she was supposed to be the protector from locusts. With so much defeat, Pharaoh's power had been challenged to the point of a compromise, but as time passed, he once again refused the petition of Moses.

The ninth plague was that of **Darkness** (Exodus 10:21–29). The plague of darkness attacked six Egyptian gods, Re, Amon-re, Aten, Atum, and Horus the Egyptian sun gods. Included in this attack was Thoth, the Egyptian moon god. This plague did not impact the Hebrews, as while darkness was over Egypt, light was in the land of Goshen and the Hebrews.

It should be noted that none of the nine plagues were uncommon in Egypt, but what made it unusual was they all occurred when God ordained as Moses foretold the occurrence of the different plagues. The exact nature and the severity could not be matched by the Egyptian wise men, sorcerers and magicians, except for the first two.

After suffering the effects of nine plagues over possibly ten months or more, the Lord is about to show His supremacy in the tenth and final plague, the **Death of the Firstborn** (Exodus 12:29–36). This was a judgment and a final assault on all of the Egyptian gods, including Pharaoh who saw himself as the supreme god. This attack and defeat would also show complete power over the Egyptian god, Osiris, considered to be the giver of life.

Pharaoh believed he was the god of all gods, and his first son also accepted he was a god the same as his father. Pharaoh challenged Moses that he was greater than the God of the Hebrews. A previous Pharaoh had killed the sons of the

Hebrews many years before, now 80 years on, God would kill the firstborn sons of the Egyptians. In the future it would be written, *"Vengeance is Mine, says the Lord. I will repay."* Leviticus 19:18, Deuteronomy 32:35, Romans 12:19

   Pharaoh had entertained the works of Moses and his God and told Moses if he saw him again, he would die. No more challengers and defeats. In this word of Pharaoh, he had set the scene for the final plague that would be a challenge for both the Hebrews and the Egyptians. The one advantage the Hebrews had was the inside information given to them by the Lord through Moses. Moses outlined what would take place, then left the presence of Pharaoh in great anger. Exodus 11:2–8

   The Lord had previously revealed to Moses what would be the final outcome. When Moses stood before the unconsumed burning bush in Midian, after he had accepted the plan and purpose of the Lord, the Lord said:

> *"When you go back to Egypt, see that you do all those wonders before Pharaoh which I have put in your hand. But I will harden his heart, so that he will not let the people go. Then you shall say to Pharaoh, 'Thus says the Lord: "Israel is My son, My firstborn. So I say to you, let My son go that he may serve Me. But if you refuse to let him go, indeed I will kill your son, your firstborn"'."*
>
> Exodus 4:21–23

The tenth plague was the turning point for the Hebrews. Up until now, they had endured hardship and experienced only the first three plagues, but the tide had turned as only the Egyptians experienced the annoyance and devastation of their gods. Through Moses, the Israelites were called to complete obedience. If they did not comply with God's directive it meant certain death.

Protection accompanied obedience, but to accept this partnership meant following precisely what Father God ordained. In the fullness of time, the time had arrived to call this nation to Himself, to become His chosen race and worship Him only. While they saw a land flowing with milk and honey, the reality was the challenge to obey what God was about to ordain.

Moses outlined the procedures to be followed. This was a new directive as nothing had ever been suggested or completed like this in the past. They had no idea of what everything meant, but only that what was about to happen would remain a memorial or testament to the God of Abraham, Isaac and Jacob, and the promises given in the distant past.

Moses issued the following instructions to be meticulously carried out. The selection of an unblemished male lamb under the age of one year which was to be separated for four days from the rest. To be killed and roasted on the fourth day at twilight, eaten with bitter herbs and unleavened bread. They were to be completely dressed and ready to leave while they participated in this meal, and were to remain inside the house until morning.

The Third Forty Years

Some of the blood of the slain lamb, with the aid of hyssop, was to be applied to the side posts and the lintel of the door.

Moses spoke of the Lord passing over them only if this was completed. Were these people any different to those in the days of Noah whom he shared with about rain coming downward not up from the ground? As I pondered these thoughts, I wondered if some of the Hebrews failed to comply with the directive of God through Moses and suffered the same fate as the Egyptians? We are not told.

Many other instructions were given to Moses regarding the Passover and the days that followed. Unleavened bread was to be eaten for seven days and only those who were circumcised could partake. The firstborn male was consecrated to God along with all firstborn animals. This was to be remembered as the Lord's Day, by His strong hand He delivered Israel from bondage. Exodus 13:1–10

While the Hebrews stayed within their homes and roasted the whole complete lamb over the fire, then shared the meal, fully dressed, unleavened bread and bitter herbs the only accompaniment to the lamb, the Lord moved over the land of Egypt. Not even a dog barked as the Lord mysteriously implemented what Moses had prophesied to Pharaoh. Exodus 11:7

The time was about midnight when the Lord struck all the firstborns in the land of Egypt except in Goshen. Not a house was spared, even the palace where the firstborn son of Pharaoh had died. Pharaoh called Moses and Aaron by night and said,

> *"Rise, go out from among my people,*
> *both you and the children of Israel.*
> *And go, serve the Lord as you have said.*
> *Also take your flocks and your herds,*
> *as you have said, and be gone;*
> *and bless me also."*
>
> Exodus 12:31–32

Pharaoh was directly touched by this final plague. He requested that the children of Israel leave and also asked for a blessing. At this point, Pharaoh acknowledged the God of the Hebrews was God and that he and the gods of Egypt were defeated.

As the children of Israel left, they plundered the Egyptians for the Lord had previously said this was to be carried out (Exodus 11:2). Gold, silver and clothes were given without incident, as all were content to watch as the Hebrews left to have their days of worship and sacrifice. About six hundred men on foot, besides children and a mixed multitude which totalled somewhere between one and a half million to two million souls were led out by Moses. Four hundred and thirty years had passed since the arrival of Jacob and his families. The first promise was well on its way to completion, that being a mighty nation, but two more promises were yet to be fulfilled.

The Third Forty Years

> *"So God led the people around*
> *by the way of the wilderness of the Red Sea.*
> *And the children of Israel went up*
> *in orderly ranks out of the land of Egypt."*
>
> Exodus 13:18

The Israelites left Egypt in an orderly fashion which meant they were organised and in fighting formation. God's people were not disorganised and panic-stricken, fleeing for their lives. Moses remembered to take the bones of Joseph with them, because of the solemn oath their ancestors had agreed to, that when the day finally came for Israel, as a nation to leave Egypt, his remains were to go with them.

As they proceeded orderly out of Pharaoh's presence and Egypt, the Lord went before them.

> *"And the Lord went before them*
> *by day in a pillar of cloud to lead the way,*
> *and by night in a pillar of fire to give them light,*
> *so as to go by day and night.*
> *He did not take away the pillar of cloud by day*
> *or the pillar of fire by night from before the people."*
>
> Exod. 13:21–22

The Children of Israel left Succoth and camped in Etham at the edge of the wilderness. Although we are not told, this would have been a great time and place for Moses to outline what God had ordained for them, while the pillar of cloud would provide guidance and protection for them all. Isaiah wrote a verse to bring clarity to their situation when he said:

> *"Then the Lord will create above*
> *every dwelling place of Mount Zion,*
> *and above her assemblies,*
> *a cloud and smoke by day*
> *and the shining of flaming fire by night.*
> *For over all the glory there will be a covering."*
>
> Isaiah 4:5

This verse describes the conditions of protection, guidance, and divine glory that prevailed during the wilderness journeys of Israel (Exod. 40:34–38). God is providing Protection, Presence, and Provision for these people as they moved across a hot steamy desert, the pillar of cloud by day protected them from the scorching sun and the pillar of fire gave them warmth from the freezing temperatures found only in the desert at night. This was a massive cloud that covered the whole assembly, which moved and they followed, until reaching their destination. They continued to travel, day and night until the cloud stopped. Following under the cloud of covering, the people camped in Etham (Exodus 13:20). Sometime after, the cloud moved and they camped by the Red Sea at Pi Hahiroth. Exodus 14:9

Pharaoh had sought a blessing from Moses' God after admitting defeat. He believed what Moses had asked, and became concerned that they had become lost (Exodus 14:3). Pharaoh was a broken man but this all changed when he was told the truth. Moses had lied and handled the truth carelessly as he hid the real reason why the Israelites wanted to leave. Pharaoh expected them to return when their worship and sacrifices were completed, but now he is remorseful of what he had allowed, frustrated, angry and wanted revenge.

When it is said that God hardened his heart, we need to remember God has given us free will. We are what the years have made us. God understood Pharaoh and knew he would react this way. God is not the God of confusion, but of peace (1 Corinthians 14:33a). He does not compel us to go against our will, He just makes us willing to obey. In the case of Pharaoh, God used his past for His glorification, for we read:

> *"Then I will harden Pharaoh's heart,*
>
> *so that he will pursue them;*
>
> *and I will gain honour over Pharaoh*
>
> *and over all his army,*
>
> *that the Egyptians may know that I am the Lord."*
>
> Exodus 14:4

With all the Israelites had witnessed and endured over the preceding months, when they saw Pharaoh and his fighting force, they thought they would die in the desert and blamed

Moses. They would die in the desert, but it would be because of their own doing, not Moses.

The place where they camped was like a trap. They had gone as far as they could, then returned to where they were. Mountain cliffs were on both sides, the Red Sea in front and Pharaoh's armies behind. The cloud moved and went between them and the army of Pharaoh.

The plague of darkness had reoccurred as the Egyptian gods of the sun and moon were targeted. Israel had light, but the Egyptians were in darkness. Their gods did not come to help the Egyptians. As Moses stretched his arm and rod over the sea, He gave the order to move forward as the cloud of protection was behind them. While they had followed the cloud, now they were commanded to move forward in faith and trust. Their hope was in their hands and attitudes. Because God had called these people, He opened the way for them as a strong east wind blew all night to clear a passage through the Red Sea. Walls of water on both sides and dry ground for them to walk and travel on.

An Egyptian chariot is at least two and a half metres long plus the front part of the horse. One chariot would be just over three and a half metres. Six hundred chariots would have stretched a long way plus the distance before and after. If they travelled in threes, plus the distance surrounding each chariot, the distance would stretch for about one kilometre. Maybe the area they travelled on was much wider than depicted. Even if the chariots were reduced to half a kilometre racing through the middle of the Red Sea passage, with distances before and after, it would have been a formidable sight to the Israelites.

Unbeknown to the Israelites, God provided for their preservation and His glory.

"The Lord looked down upon the army of the Egyptians through the pillar of fire and cloud, and He troubled (confused) the army of the Egyptians."

Exodus 14:24

After sufficient time had passed for freedom to be gained, the cloud of darkness lifted, which revealed the absence of the Hebrews. In a confused state, the Egyptian army pursued the children of Israel, but to no avail, as the wheels fell off the choice chariots. And they said, *"Let us flee from the face of Israel, for the Lord fights for them against the Egyptians"* (v26). But the Lord said to Moses, *"Stretch out your hand over the sea, that the waters may come back upon the Egyptians, on their chariots, and on their horsemen. Then the waters returned and covered the chariots, the horsemen and all the army of Pharaoh. Not so much as one of them remained."* Exodus 14:27–28

The sight on the following morning of their crossing must have been one to behold. As the Israelites looked from the opposite side of the Red Sea to where only a few hours before they had stood, trembling for their lives, the dead bodies of men and animals, debris from chariots, strewn along the shoreline, must have been a stark reminder of the God who was on their side. Life had changed so quickly for this favoured people of God. Responsibilities they needed to embrace, moving from slavery to freedom, now confronted them. Life for them had indeed changed in an instant, but were they ready for the unexpected?

But there is also another side of this coin that should be embraced. What about the Egyptian mothers and wives now left without a husband or father? Fatherless children, and responsibilities for care and home that were completed previously by the Hebrew women or slaves. So many dead. Their religion and beliefs were ripped to pieces in a few short months. Mothers who had grieved for their firstborn continued to grieve for the loss of their husbands. How these people were caught up in decisions made, not of their choosing, but they wore the consequences of those in power. Is there a lesson within this tragedy for us to learn from?

There is a verse of scripture that I would share with you concerning the ways and mind of Father God.

> *"For My thoughts are not your thoughts,*
> *nor are My ways," says the Lord.*
> *"For as the heavens are higher than the earth,*
> *so are My ways higher than your ways,*
> *and My thoughts than your thoughts."*
>
> Isaiah 55:8–9

The Third Forty Years

The cloud was moving again. These children of Israel were travelling forward to acquire the promises given so many years previous. One could imagine the questions being rumoured amongst themselves. Where are we going? Where is this promised land and what does it hold for us? Had any counted the cost of how they would survive and how long the journey would take? I am sure there were many other thoughts at this time. So many questions. So few answers.

It wasn't very long before their hoarded resources ran out. Water became short in supply and the children of Israel complained (Exodus 15:24). It was at Marah, that God made the bitter waters sweet as they were introduced to obedience to God (Exodus 15:25–26). After having camped at Elim where there were twelve wells of water and seventy palm trees, they now moved out into the Wilderness of Sin (Exodus 16:1). Again, the people complained, as they remembered the foods they ate back in Egypt, as they now faced hunger.

Meat and bread were provided but not as they expected (Exodus 16:12–14). Manna is introduced to these complainers. Little did these people realise, the six-day gathering of this seed (Exodus 16:31), would be a discipline as the chosen people of God, would endure for over forty years (Exodus 16:35). They also complained about water at Rephidim (Exodus 17:1) and God told Moses to:

"Go on before the people,
and take with you some of the elders of Israel.

Also take in your hand your rod with you.

Behold I will stand before you there on the rock in Horeb;

and you shall strike the rock,

and water will come out of it, that the people may drink."

Exodus 17:5–6

In Egypt, the Israelites complained about the harshness of their work, but now it was about fundamentals. Their despair is evident in the fact that they are ready to stone Moses, as they had stopped trusting God and were looking to Moses the man as their source and provider. Many years later, Jesus would correct the thinking of the people of His day when He supplied the five thousand with bread and fish. They wanted to make Him king, and as they looked to Jesus to supply their need, He told them it was all about the Father, not Him or Moses as their ancestors presumed. John 6:22–33

The Amalekites saw Israel as an easy target. This nomadic tribe were descendants of Amalek, the grandson of Esau, the older brother of Jacob. When they attacked Israel, Moses was quick to react as he chose Joshua to select some men to wage war with this distant group of relatives. Moses assured Joshua he would be his support as he ventured out to show the hand of God's protection. Moses, Aaron and Hur went up to the top of the hill that overlooked the battle site. While Moses held his hand up, Israel prevailed, but when his hand came down, Amalek prevailed.

Because Moses became tired, a stone was bought for him to sit on and his arms were supported by Aaron and Hur until the going down of the sun. As Joshua defeated Amalek and his people with the sword, Moses built an altar and called its name, *'The-Lord-Is-My-Banner'* because the Lord had said to Moses that He would blot out the remembrance of Amalek from under heaven. Exodus 17:8–16

Moses was about to experience an unexpected event that would bring joy, peace, happiness and understanding when dealing with the problems of the Israelites.

> *"Jethro, the priest of Midian, Moses' father-in-law,*
> *heard of all that God had done for*
> *Moses and for Israel His people.*
> *Then Jethro took Zipporah, Moses' wife,*
> *after he had sent her back, with her two sons.*
> *Jethro came with Moses' wife and two sons in the wilderness,*
> *where Moses was encamped at the mountain of God."*
>
> Exodus 18:1, 2, 5

Jethro was a priest of Midian. The Midianites were descended from Abraham through his second wife Keturah who had six sons. While they believed the same as Abraham when Abraham died, so did their beliefs. Like many others, their beliefs adopted the gods of their surroundings. Midian had taken on Baal worship along with many other gods. What had happened through Moses was somewhat of a wake-up call for this priest, as his confession changed to the following.

> *"Now I know that the Lord is greater than all the gods;*
> *for in the very thing in which they behaved proudly,*
> *He was above them."*
>
> Exodus 18:11

Moses dealt with all the disputes of Israel, as they asked for the direction of the Lord. Moses was the only one familiar with the statutes of God and His laws, so Jethro provided Moses with some great counsel that it was time for him to delegate some of the responsibility. While those appointed would handle most disputes, the more difficult cases would be dealt with by Moses. Moses was teachable and listened to Jethro, and appointed many to judge the people. Jethro bid his son-in-law goodbye and headed back to his home in Midian.

Almost three months had passed and the children of Israel were camped in the wilderness before Mt. Sinai. The Lord called to Moses so he left the camp and made his way up the mountain. The Lord said to Moses:

> *"If you will indeed obey My voice*
> *and keep My covenant,*
> *then you shall be a special treasure to Me*
> *above all people; for all the earth is Mine.*

> *And you shall be to Me a kingdom of priests*
> *and a holy nation."*
>
> Exodus 19:5–6

Moses left the presence of the Lord and shared what he had been told with the elders who, along with all the people agreed when they said, *"All the Lord has spoken we will do."* Moses relayed to the Lord all the words of the people so the people consecrated themselves and changed their clothes to be clean before the Lord.

> *"On the third day, in the morning,*
> *there were thunderings and lightnings,*
> *and a thick cloud on the mountain."*
>
> Exodus 19:16a

The people went out of the camp to meet with the Lord and they stood at the foot of the mountain. When the Lord called to Moses, he went up to meet with Him. After a stern warning to Moses about the people disobeying, the Lord spoke to the whole congregation and gave them the Law of God, His Ten Commandments.

After this, the Lord called to Moses saying:

> *"Come up to Me on the mountain and be there;*
> *and I will give you tablets of stone,*

> *and the law and commandments which I have written,*
> *that you may teach them."*
>
> Exodus. 24:12

Moses spoke to the elders and told them to wait for their return as Aaron and Hur would address any difficulty that may occur. Moses, along with his assistant Joshua, went up the mountain of God where a cloud covered them, and they were on the mountain forty days and forty nights. During this time, much of the intricacies of what God had ordained were outlined to Moses including all that was to be completed when building 'The Tabernacle' and the various parts contained within.

> *"When He had made an end of speaking*
> *with him on Mount Sinai,*
> *He gave Moses two tablets of the testimony,*
> *tablets of stone, written with the finger of God."*
>
> Exodus 31:18

Moses had left his older brother Aaron and Hur with the decision-making. It wasn't long before Aaron was tested, for we read:

> *Now when the people saw that Moses*
> *delayed coming down from the mountain,*
> *the people gathered together to Aaron,*

and said to him,
"Come, make us gods that shall go before us;
for this Moses,
the man who bought us up out of Egypt,
we do not know what has become of him."

Exodus 32:1

Aaron's answer to the grumbling Israelites was to:

"Break off the golden earrings
which are in the ears of your wives,
your sons, and your daughters,
and bring them to me."
"And Aaron received the gold from their hand,
and he fashioned it with an engraving tool,
and made a molded calf."

Exodus 32:2, 4a

The Lord had spoken directly to the children of Israel when He said:

"You shall not make anything to be with Me,
gods of silver or gods of gold
you shall not make for yourselves."

Exodus 20:23

The Israelite's intention was not to reject Yahweh but wanted to worship Yahweh under the name of Apis. What does this mean? They wanted to worship God on their terms. They wanted to create a God who was a puppet, Him being subject to them, not them to Him and His demands of obedience. They wanted to live their lives doing their own thing, their way. They had successfully broken the covenant within a few days.

The Lord knew what had transpired in the Israelite camp in the absence of Moses, that they had corrupted themselves. The Lord told Moses He would destroy this wayward people, but Moses interceded for the people and reasoned with the Lord as to His decision of wrath. *So the Lord relented from the harm which He said He would do to His people.* Exodus 32:14.

Moses left the presence of the Lord to return to the Israelite camp, as he carried the tablets. Joshua remarked to Moses that there appeared to be war in the camp, but Moses said:

> *"It is not the noise of the shout of victory,*
> *nor the noise of the cry of defeat,*
> *but the sound of singing I hear."*
>
> Exodus 32:18

When Moses came near the camp, he saw the calf and the dancing which enraged him to the point where he threw the tablets and they broke into pieces at the foot of the mountain. Moses challenged Aaron as to why this took place. Aaron replied, *"Do not let the anger of my lord become hot. You know the people,*

> *that they are set on evil. For they said to me, 'Make us gods that shall go before us; as for this Moses, the man who brought us out of the land of Egypt, we do not know what has become of him.' And I said to them, 'Whoever has any gold, let them break it off.' So, they gave it to me, and I cast it into the fire, and this calf came out."* Exodus 32:21–24

If this wasn't so sad it would be funny. A guilty person will do anything except the one thing that he or she is required to do, and that is to confess and repent. When Aaron was confronted by Moses, he never denied the wrong, never, not one time, but merely tried to explain it away. The Lord was not amused by Aaron's excuse as He wanted to destroy the entire Israelite community.

Moses knew the depth of sin these people had committed, so he returned to the Lord and interceded for them by offering his own life in exchange for theirs (Exodus 32:32). Father God was sympathetic to Moses and told him to go back and lead them to the place He had spoken to him about. The Lord told Moses that His Angel would continue to go before them all. When Moses related what the Lord had said about them being a stiff-necked people, they mourned and took off all their ornaments at Mount Horeb.

Moses took his tent and pitched it outside the camp and called it the *'Tabernacle of Meeting'*.

> *"So it was, whenever Moses went out to the tabernacle,*
> *that all the people rose,*

> *and each man stood at his tent door and watched Moses until he had gone into the tabernacle. Then a pillar of cloud descended and stood at the door of the tabernacle, and the Lord talked with Moses."*
>
> Exodus 33:8–9

Moses left the Tabernacle of Meeting, but Joshua, a young man remained inside (Exodus 33:11). As Moses and the Lord communed together, Moses understood that he had found grace in the sight of the Lord. He asked the Lord to show him His glory, but was told that no one could see His face and live, so, Moses was given an alternative.

"Here is a place by Me, and you shall stand on the rock. So it shall be, while My glory passes by, that I will put you in the cleft of the rock, and will cover you with My hand while I pass by. Then I will take away my hand and you shall see My back; but My face shall not be seen." Exodus 33:21–23

Moses prepared two new tablets and presented himself to the Lord and renewed the covenant that had been previously made. When Moses came down from the mountain carrying the new tablets, the people noticed his face shone, and they were afraid. But Moses shared with them all that the Lord had taught him, then covered his face with a veil. Whenever he spoke with the Lord, he would remove the veil, but when reunited with the Israelites, he would use the veil.

Moses spoke to all the congregation of the children of Israel, about a freewill offering for the building of the Tabernacle and all the various parts.

> *"Then everyone came whose heart was stirred,*
> *and everyone whose spirit was willing,*
> *and they brought the Lord's offering*
> *for the work of the tabernacle of meeting,*
> *for all its service, and for the holy garments."*
>
> Exodus 35:21

It was time to build the Tabernacle so Artisans were called. The grandson of Hur of the tribe of Judah was called whose name was Bezalel. Moses told the children of Israel,

> *"God has filled Bezalel with the Spirit of God,*
> *in wisdom and understanding,*
> *in knowledge and all manner of workmanship."*
> *"And he has put in his heart the ability to teach,*
> *and Aholiab of the tribe of Dan."*
>
> Exodus 35:31, 34

Each day the people brought everything that was required for this God-ordained work to be completed. So generous were the people that Moses restrained the people from bringing as sufficient had been offered, indeed too much. With more than enough to proceed, the work began. Ten curtains woven of fine linen, of blue, purple, and scarlet thread. The Ark of the Covenant, the Showbread Table, the Golden Lampstand, and the Altar of Incense were all made with acacia wood overlaid with gold.

The Bronze Altar of Burnt Offerings, the Bronze Laver, along with all the utensils were made. The Court of the Tabernacle was constructed also the Priesthood Garments. The Ephod was special as was the Breastplate, as jewels were added to adorn these special pieces of clothing. Many other Priestly garments were made for Aaron and his sons. A turban of fine linen, exquisite hats of fine linen. *Then they made the plate of the holy crown of pure gold, and wrote on it an inscription like the engraving of a signet:*

"HOLINESS TO THE LORD."

Exodus 39:30

When all the work had been completed, according to all that the Lord had commanded Moses, the children of Israel brought everything to Moses. *Then Moses looked over all the work, and indeed they had done it; as the Lord had commanded, just so they had done it. And Moses blessed them.* Exodus 39:43

The Lord met with Moses and outlined when and how the Tabernacle was to be set up. (Exodus 40:1–33). When everything was in place:

> *"The cloud covered the tabernacle of meeting,
> and the glory of the Lord filled the tabernacle."*
>
> Exodus 40:34

> *As the children of Israel continued to camp at Mount Sinai,
> the cloud of the Lord was above the tabernacle by day, and
> fire was over it by night, in the sight of all the house of
> Israel, throughout all their journey.*
>
> Exodus 40:38

Moses was called to teach the Israelites much that the Lord had told Him previously. He taught about the sacrificial system, the service of the priests in the sanctuary, the laws governing impurities, holiness codes and gifts to the sanctuary. For more in-depth teaching about each of these subjects, please consult the Book of Leviticus.

Not everything goes according to what a person thinks or understands about a situation or what Father God had ordained. Two sons of Aaron, Nadab and Abihu, took their censer and put fire in it, and offered profane fire before the Lord, which He had not commanded them. *The fire went out from the Lord and devoured them, and they died before the Lord* (Leviticus 10:2). Moses said to Aaron, *"This is what the Lord spoke, saying:*

'By those who come near Me
I must be regarded as holy;
and before all the people
I must be glorified'."

Leviticus 10:3b

Although Aaron held his peace, the Lord was required to warn Aaron through Moses about wrong understanding.

"Tell Aaron your brother not to come
at just any time into the Holy Place inside the veil,
before the ark, lest he die;
for I will appear in the cloud above the mercy seat."

Leviticus 16:2

God did not play favourites. This was the *Day of Atonement* which was to be observed in the proper ordained fashion according to the law God had set down. Nothing else was acceptable. The Day of Atonement was observed on one day of the year, not when anyone felt like it. God had certainly shown grace to Aaron. Slowly but surely the children of Israel were schooled in the things of God and what the covenant meant that they had agreed to.

Two years had passed since Moses had led the children of Israel out of captivity to the Egyptians. The Lord spoke to Moses in the Wilderness of Sinai, in the tabernacle of meeting, that a census of all the congregation should be taken. This was to be carried out in the following fashion.

- By their families, by their fathers' houses, according to the number of names, every male individually.
- From twenty years old and above, all who can go to war in Israel.
- Moses and Aaron shall number them by their armies.
- A man from every tribe, each one the head of his father's house.

The Lord appointed the Levites to dismantle and assemble the *Tabernacle* at God's appointed time, all others faced death. The Lord also ordained,

"The children of Israel shall pitch their tents, everyone by his own camp, everyone by his own standard, according to their armies; but the Levites shall camp around the Tabernacle of the Testimony, that there may be no wrath on the congregation of the children of Israel; and the Levites shall keep charge of the Tabernacle of the Testimony."

The children did all according to all the Lord commanded Moses. Numbers 1:52–54

The camp was set out in the following way.

- North:
  Dan (62,700), Asher (41,500), Naphatali (53, 400).
- South:
  Reuben (46,500), Simeon (59,300), Gad ($5, 650).
- East:
  Judah (74,600), Issachar (54,400), Zebulun (57, 400).
- West:
  Ephraim (40,500), Manasseh (32,200), Benjamin (35,400).

Moses was familiar with another group of people who chose to be part of a priestly group who served but were not necessarily Levites. Early in the history of Israel, the Lord established the Nazarites as a unique category of people. They chose to be devoted to His service for an unspecified time. Nazarites embraced both men and women from the Israelite community, some for life, while others chose a short or longer term. (Numbers 6:1–27). The Lord gave a special blessing to Moses who instructed Aaron and his sons how they would bless the children of Israel. This is known as the *Nazarite Blessing*.

> *"The Lord bless you and keep you;*
> *The Lord make His face shine upon you,*
> *and be gracious to you;*
> *The Lord lift up His countenance upon you,*
> *and give you peace."*
>
> Numbers 6:24–26

The Lord spoke to Moses in the Wilderness of Sinai, in the first month of the second year after they had come out of the land of Egypt, that they were required to keep the Passover at its appointed time. As this is recorded as the second Passover, Egypt as the first, then the year before was not commemorated as the Israelites were anticipating to be in the promised land where this would be celebrated. *"While man plans his way, God directs his steps."* Proverbs 16:9

The Lord had told Moses that the movement of the Cloud or Fire would be the signal to break camp or move as was directed. The children of Israel knew their stay could be two days, a month, a year or longer, as their movement was totally at the Lord's discretion. If the cloud didn't move, then they remained encamped wherever they were.

The children of Israel had observed the Passover celebrations on the fourteenth day of the second month. On the twentieth day of the second month, the cloud was taken up and the Israelites knew it was time to move on. They left the Wilderness of Sin and settled in the Wilderness of Paran, some three days journey. Numbers 10:33

As the Lord was leading the children of Israel forward to another destination, Moses told his brother-in-law Hobab and asked him to join with them, to accompany them for the Lord had promised good things to Israel. But Hobab told Moses that he would depart and return to his own land and to his relatives. Moses pleaded with him to stay as he said:

> *"Please do not leave, inasmuch as you know*
> *how we are to camp in the wilderness,*
> *and you can be my eyes.*
> *And it shall be, if you go with us,*
> *indeed it shall be,*
> *that whatever good the Lord will do to us,*
> *the same we will do to you."*
>
> Numbers 10:29–32

Moses was feeling the pressure of leadership, even though the Lord had called him, as the constant complaining of the people had worn him down. The Israelites had been camped in one place for about two years when they were told to pack up and move. When they settled into their new surroundings, old habits came to the surface and the children of Israel complained.

There were also a group, a mixed multitude who left Egypt in the Exodus. They cried out to Moses about all the things they had previously and now were somewhat vegetarians, as only manna was provided. They did have their cattle, sheep and goats, but not the cucumbers, melons, leeks, onions, and garlic. Their bodies had dried up and they were discontented.

Moses took his plea to the Lord, and the Lord heard and replied to his predicament. Moses was to gather to the Lord seventy men of the elders of the people and officers over them and bring them to the Tabernacle of Meeting. The Lord told Moses he would endow them with the same Spirit as he had. After the men had consecrated themselves, the Spirit of the Lord rested on them and they prophesied, but only this once.

Two others were supposed to go up, but Eldad and Medad did not, although they prophesied in the camp. When Joshua heard about this he said, *"Moses my lord, forbid them!"* But Moses replied, *"Are you zealous for my sake? Oh, that all the Lord's people were prophets and that the Lord would put His Spirit upon them!"* Numbers 11:28–29

The Lord answered the petition of Moses and told him that He would supply the whole camp with meat, not for one day but a month until it became loathsome to them. While Moses did not know how the Lord would provide, he believed. The Lord sent a wind that brought quail from the sea fluttering near the camp to a distance of about a day's journey. The people gathered many for themselves. But while the meat was still between their teeth, the Lord sent a great plague and killed all those who had yielded to cravings.

Moses became accustomed to dealing with people who grumbled, but when the attack came from within the family, the Lord did not abandon Moses. Miriam and Aaron, the older sister and brother, challenged Moses to the legitimacy of Moses as the mouthpiece of the Lord because he had married a non-Israelite. They questioned and suggested that they too could speak for the Lord.

> *Suddenly the Lord said to Moses,*
> *Aaron and Miriam, "Come out, you three,*
> *to the Tabernacle of Meeting!"*
> *So the three came out.*
>
> Numbers 12:4

The Lord then outlined to all three how He called, saw and acknowledged Moses. The Lord certainly went before Moses and protected him. The anger of the Lord was aroused against Miriam and Aaron, and when the cloud departed from the Tabernacle, Miriam was leprous, as white as snow. When Aaron noticed the condition of his sister, he pleaded for forgiveness on their behalf saying they had acted foolishly and sinned. Moses cried out to the Lord, saying, *"Please heal her, O God, I pray!"* Miriam was removed from the camp for seven days then returned, healed.

The children of Israel camped at Kadesh Barnea on the border of the Wilderness of Paran and the Wilderness of Zin. Expectations were running high as they had arrived, and the promised land was within their grasp.

> *The Lord spoke to Moses saying,*
> *"Send men to spy out the land of Canaan,*
> *which I am giving to the children of Israel"*
>
> Numbers 13:2a

Moses received word from the Lord that it was time to send out spies into the land of Canaan and bring back a report. Twelve headmen were chosen, one from each tribe. They were:

- The tribe of Reuben, Shammua.
- The tribe of Simeon, Shaphat.
- The tribe of Judah, Caleb.
- The tribe of Issachar, Igal.
- The tribe of Ephraim, Joshua.
- The tribe of Benjamin, Palti.
- The tribe of Zebulun, Gaddiel.
- The tribe of Manasseh, Gaddi.
- The tribe of Dan, Ammiel.
- The tribe of Asher, Sethur.
- The tribe of Naphtali, Nahbi.
- The tribe of Gad, Geuel.

Moses told the men to observe whether the people were strong or weak, few or many. Was the land rich or poor? Did the people live in strongholds or tents, and if there were forests? Moses also suggested they bring back some fruit of the land (Numbers 13:17–20). Forty days later they returned (Numbers 13:25), but what had they seen?

Only two out of twelve spies saw with the eyes of the Lord, Joshua and Caleb. Two walked in faith, while the others walked in fear.

Caleb brought order to the people when the ten bad reports were told, he said:

> *"Let us go up at once and take possession,*
> *for we are well able to overcome it."*
>
> Numbers 13:30

The bad reports impacted the Israelites to the point where they lifted their voices and cried all night. Once again, the children of Israel complained against Moses and Aaron saying they should have died in the land of Egypt. They further questioned as they believed they would die in battle and become victims.

> *So they said to one another,*
> *"Let us select a leader and return to Egypt."*
>
> Numbers 14:4

Joshua and Caleb both addressed the congregation with positive words as to the Lord delighting in them Who will give them the land He had promised. The people are their bread for the Lord has removed their protection and will allow the Israelites to be victorious, only don't rebel against the Lord now, at this time. But the congregation threatened Joshua and Caleb with stoning. As the people watched, the glory of the Lord appeared in the Tabernacle of Meeting before the children of Israel.

The Third Forty Years

When all seems lost, the Lord intervenes, never early or late. Because of the ten, the Lord brought swift judgment on these people. They had disobeyed and rejected God's plans for them. *Then the Lord said to Moses: "How long will these people reject Me? And how long will they not believe Me, with all the signs which I have performed among them?"* (Numbers 14:11). Ten times the Lord had accused the Israelites of testing Him. As a refusal to go into the promised land was the tenth, what were the other nine?

1. Lack of faith before the Red Sea crossing.
   Exodus. 14:11–12

2. Complaining about the bitter water at Marah.
   Exodus 15:24

3. Complaining in the Desert of Sin.
   Exodus 16:3

4. Collecting more manna than told.
   Exodus 16:20

5. Attempting to collect manna on the Sabbath.
   Exodus 16:27–29

6. Complaining about the lack of water at Rephidim.
   Exodus 17:2–3

7. Engaging in idolatry in the golden calf.
   Exodus 32:7–10

8. Complaining at Taberah.
   Numbers 11:1–2

9. Complaining over the lack of food.
   Numbers 11:4

10. Failing to trust God to enter the Promised Land.
    Numbers 14:1–4

Moses is very aware of the anger the Israelites have kindled before the Lord, and so interceded again on their behalf. He appealed to the grace of God, not the law of God for he says,

> *"The Lord is longsuffering and abundant in mercy,*
>
> *forgiving iniquity and transgression;*
>
> *but He by no means clears the guilty,*
>
> *visiting the iniquity of the fathers on the children*
>
> *to the third and fourth generation."*
>
> Numbers 14:18

The Lord replied, *"Because all these men who have seen My glory and the signs which I did in Egypt and in the wilderness, and have put me to the test now these ten times, and not heeded My voice, they certainly shall not see the land of which I swore to their fathers, nor shall any of those who reject Me see it."* Numbers 14:22–23

The Lord had passed the death sentence on the rebels. The only exceptions were Caleb, because he had a different spirit in him and had followed the Lord faithfully (Numbers 14:24a), and Joshua. Only these two would enter the promised land, as the other ten, who brought a bad report died by a plague before the Lord.

The Third Forty Years

The Israelites recognised they had sinned before the Lord, and gathered to do what was required at first and go into the promised land. But decisions made carry consequences. The Lord had already cast judgment on the people, to now do anything else would be to transgress the command of the Lord as His protection had been withdrawn against the enemies. Even with this information, the people went up and were defeated by the Amalekites and the Canaanites and fell by the sword. The ark of the covenant of the Lord nor Moses departed from the camp.

Moses continued to teach the children of Israel what God had set out in His covenant with them. But lurking in the background were always those who thought they knew better and chose to be equal or above God's appointed, Moses. Korah, Dathan, Abiram, and On took men and two hundred and fifty representatives and leaders of the congregation, men of renown, and rose before Moses and Aaron saying that they exalted themselves more than they should.

As this was a challenge against the Lord, He brought swift judgment on them. Those who were accused were told to separate themselves from the others. When this was completed, the Lord opened up the ground and swallowed them all alive, into the pit then closed the ground over again. The two hundred and fifty who were offering incense were consumed by fire. Only a descendant of Aaron was to offer incense to the Lord.

But the complaining was not over. The next day Moses was accused of killing the people of the Lord. The anger of the Lord was aroused again against those who complained. As Moses was aware of what had happened, he told Aaron to take a censer, put fire in it from the altar, and sprinkle incense on it. Aaron did what he was told and stood in the middle of the congregation. This would make an atonement for these people, but the plague had begun, so Aaron stood between the dead and the living which stopped the plague, but not before fourteen thousand seven hundred died. This did not include those who died on the previous day in the Korah incident. Numbers 15:1–16:49

The Lord provided a solution to the complaints that were constantly aimed at Moses. A rod of the leader of each of the twelve tribes was to have their name on the rod and brought to Moses where he would place them in the Tabernacle. This was completed, so the Lord would show who He had chosen as priest. The next day, the rod of Aaron, of the house of Levi, had sprouted and put forth buds, had produced blossoms and yielded ripe almonds.

The Lord had chosen the tribe who would be His priests, who would attend to all the needs of the Tabernacle and the sanctuary. The Lord said:

> *"Behold, I Myself have taken your brethren*
> *the Levites from among the children of Israel;*
> *they are a gift to you, given by the Lord,*
> *to do the work of the tabernacle of meeting."*
>
> Numbers 18:6

Therefore you and your sons with you shall attend to your priesthood for everything at the altar and behind the veil; and you shall serve (Numbers 18:17a). Moses continued his teaching relating to the priests, their duties and their care.

Miriam, the sister of Moses died in Kadesh, and they buried her there. But the children of Israel once again found themselves without water so they complained about Moses leading them to an evil place where they would die. They complained that it was not a place of grain, figs, vines or pomegranates. So Moses and Aaron sought guidance at the Tabernacle of Meeting from the Lord. Then the Lord spoke to Moses, saying,

"Take the rod; you and your brother Aaron
gather the congregation together.
Speak to the rock before their eyes,
and it will yield its water;
thus you shall bring water for them out of the rock,
and give drink to the congregation and their animals."

Numbers 20:8

For whatever reason, Moses did not hear the directions or commands of the Lord. Moses spoke sternly to the congregation which he called rebels, then struck the rock twice with his rod, and water came out abundantly, so the congregation and the animals drank. Father God was not at all pleased with what Moses had done, so he spoke to him saying:

> *"Because you did not believe Me,*
> *to hallow Me in the eyes of the children of Israel,*
> *therefore you shall not bring this assembly*
> *into the land which I have given them."*
>
> Numbers 20:12

Moses sent messengers to the king of Edom asking to pass through their land as they would only use the King's Highway. Moses referred to Edom as a brother to Israel. Edom was a descendant of Esau, the brother of Jacob. After two failed attempts to negotiate a peaceful journey, Moses travelled to Mount Hor by the border of the land of Edom.

Aaron's time to depart this world was made known to Moses. The Lord told Moses to take Aaron and Eleazar and bring them up to Mount Hor where Moses would remove the vestments from Aaron and put them on Eleazar. After this was completed, Aaron died and Moses and Eleazar came back down the mountain. When the congregation saw that Aaron was dead, all the houses of Israel mourned for Aaron for thirty days. Numbers 20:29

The conquest of the promised land was in progress. As Moses travelled the road to Atharim, the Canaanites fought against Israel and took some of them prisoners, but after Israel had made a vow to the Lord, they attacked the Canaanites and utterly destroyed them and their cities. Numbers 21:1–3

The Third Forty Years

As the way was blocked for the Israelites to proceed, they travelled to Mount Hor via the Way of the Red Sea to go around the land of Edom. But the soul of the people became very discouraged on the way. The people again spoke against the Lord and Moses.

> *"Why have you brought us up out of Egypt*
> *to die in the wilderness?*
> *For there is no food and no water,*
> *and our soul loathes this worthless bread."*
>
> Numbers 21:5

The Lord sent fiery serpents among the people, and many of the people died. As the people once again confessed their sins, they asked Moses to pray that the Lord would deliver them from the serpents. Then the Lord said to Moses:

> *"Make a fiery serpent, and set it on a pole;*
> *and it shall be that everyone who is bitten,*
> *when he looks at it, shall live."*
>
> Numbers 21:8

Moses did as he was commanded, and all those who looked at the bronze serpent lived.

Moses conducted several conquests as they travelled from Mount Hor to Moab, as the children of Israel camped in the plains of Moab on the side of the Jordan across from Jericho. Moses was not always privy to the protection or how the Lord went before them. As Israel camped, Balak sent for Balaam to curse Israel. The Lord revealed Himself to Balaam and told him that he was not to curse Israel as they were His blessed nation, but Balaam eventually obeyed the command of the Lord, through a rather diverse circumstance. Numbers 22:1–24:25

The Israelites remained in Moab at a place called Acacia Grove and began to commit harlotry with the women of Moab. The Israelites attended their sacrifices to their gods and bowed to them. The anger of the Lord was aroused against Israel because they had joined to Baal of Peor. The Lord commanded Moses to take the leaders and hang them, but while this was taking place, one of the children of Israel came and presented to his brethren a Midianite woman in the sight of Moses and the congregation who were weeping at the door of the Tabernacle of Meeting.

When Phinehas the son of Eleazar, the son of Aaron the priest saw it, he rose from among the congregation and took a javelin in his hand; and went after the man of Israel into his tent and thrust both of them through, the man of Israel, and the woman through her body. So the plague was stopped among the children of Israel. Twenty-four thousand died in the plague. Numbers 25:7–9

The Lord commanded Moses to carry out another census of Israel. When everything was completed, the first and second censuses were compared. Moses and Eleazer numbered the children of Israel in the plains of Moab by the Jordan, across from Jericho.

The Third Forty Years

> *"But among these there was not a man of those who were numbered by Moses and Aaron the priest when they numbered the children of Israel in the Wilderness of Sinai."*
>
> Numbers 26:64

Moses diligently taught the children of Israel the laws Father God had ordained, so they would understand what was expected and to obey. The offerings for the *Passover*, the *Feast of Weeks*, the *Feast of Trumpets*, the *Day of Atonement* and the *Feast of Tabernacles* were thoroughly taught so observance would be acceptable to Father God as well as other laws.

The Lord spoke to Moses and told him to take vengeance on the Medianites. The Lord also told Moses that after he had completed this last assignment, he would join his sister and brother, as he would be gathered to his people. Moses chose a thousand from each tribe to carry out the Lord's bidding. Phinehas the son of Eleazar the priest, with the holy articles and the signal trumpets, were to accompany the chosen.

All the males and the five kings were killed along with Balaam. All the women along with their little ones were taken captive, as well as their cattle, flocks and all their goods. As they left, they burned their cities as well as their forts. When the captives and all the booty were presented to Moses, he became angry that they had left the women and the children alive. Because Balaam had counselled the women to trespass against the Lord in the incident of Peor, he ordered every male killed and every female who had known a male intimately. Numbers 31:12–18

The children of Reuben and the children of Gad had a great deal of livestock and the land where they were was a suitable place for their inheritance. They asked Moses for permission to settle and not cross over the Jordan River, but Moses was not in agreeance at first, as he saw the same as their fathers did previously could take place. When they promised Moses they would build places for their wives and children to live, but the armed men would continue with the others until the land had been conquered and settled, then and only then would they return to their inheritance, Moses agreed and the deal was done.

Moses instructed the Israelites concerning their crossing of the Jordan River and their conquests that lay beyond, which included instructions to be observed and obeyed. Boundaries and leaders were made and appointed. Moses expounded more about the Law God had given to them and the adherence to obedience.

As Moses continued to teach, he summarised what he had been taught and shared the greatest commandment with the congregation.

> *"Hear, O Israel:*
> *the Lord our God, the Lord is one!*
> *You shall love the Lord your God with all your heart,*
> *with all your soul, and with all your strength."*
>
> Deuteronomy 6:4–5

Moses further encouraged the children of Israel, *"And these words which I command you today shall be in your heart. You shall teach them diligently to your children, and shall talk of them when you sit in your house, when you walk by the way, when you lie down, and when you rise up. You shall bind them as a sign on your hand, and they shall be as frontlets between your eyes. You shall write them on the doorposts on your house and on your gates."* Deuteronomy 6:6–9

Moses cautioned the Israelites about disobedience and reminded them that they were a chosen people. As they observed all that God had imparted to them, they would be blessed. They were always to remember the Lord their God and not return to the rebellious way of their predecessors, always to worship Father God and not turn to false gods or idols. Moses assured them that God would provide another prophet to take his place and that he was to be revered and obeyed as they had listened to his words and obeyed.

After Moses had assured Israel that the choice for their future was one of life or death (Deuteronomy 30:11–20), Moses reminded the Israelites that he was one hundred and twenty years old and would not cross the Jordan with them. Moses continued to encourage the Israelites when he said:

"Be strong and of good courage,
do not fear nor be afraid of them;
for the Lord your God,

He is the One who goes with you.
He will not leave you nor forsake you."

Deuteronomy 31:6

Then Moses called Joshua and said to him,

"Be strong and of good courage,
for you must go with this people to the land
which the Lord has sworn to their fathers
to give them, and you shall cause them to inherit it.
And the Lord, He is the One who goes before you.
He will be with you,
He will not leave you nor forsake you;
do not fear nor be dismayed."

Deuteronomy 31:7–8

The Lord told Moses to present Joshua and himself in the Tabernacle of Meeting so that the Lord could inaugurate him. When they came to the Tabernacle, the Lord appeared at the Tabernacle in a pillar of cloud, where the Lord shared with them both that after Moses had rested with his fathers, the people would rise and play the harlot with the gods of the foreigners. That a time would come when He would withdraw His presence from them, as they lived with their choice. After these things, the Lord inaugurated Joshua as the new leader of Israel. Deuteronomy 31:23

The Third Forty Years

Moses had lived forty years in Goshen and Egypt, then forty years in Midian where he had married Zipporah, then many years afterwards, God called Moses to lead His people out of captivity. Moses was eighty years old when he stood before Pharaoh, then after about a year, Moses led the children of Israel out of Egypt, through the Red Sea and then to Mount Sinai where he was given the law of God. Building the Tabernacle and their arrival at Kadesh-Barnea took about four years after they left Egypt.

After the refusal to go into the promised land, Moses led the children of Israel for a further thirty-five years of the forty years they were to wander in the desert. When Moses completed the second census, not one of the names of those over the age of twenty was found (Numbers 26:64). Although Moses had faltered at the second supply of water, he fulfilled the various roles of prophet, priest, ruler and saviour of Israel. Moses' most heroic virtue was in his steadfast obedience and trust in the God of his fathers, Abraham, Isaac and Jacob.

The Lord then spoke to Moses to depart and climb up Mount Nebo and there he would view the promised land that He would give the children of Israel as a possession. After a final blessing to the children of Israel, which he had taught and led for forty years, he climbed Mount Nebo and viewed the promised land, then as the Lord had said, Moses was gathered to his fathers, and the Lord buried him in a valley in the land of Moab. Deuteronomy 34:6

"A Prayer of Moses the Man of God"

As Psalm 90 is read carefully, it would appear that Moses shared this psalm as his final benediction on the life he had lived and a prayer for God's help in the coming struggles the children of Israel would face. The Lord had told both Moses and Joshua what would happen in the future with the chosen people. If only the children of Israel would listen and obey the covenant they swore to, their lives would have been secured. But as history has revealed, this was never the case.

The Path of Life

Lord, You have been our dwelling place in all generations.

Before the mountains were brought forth,

Or ever You had formed the earth and the world,

Even from everlasting to everlasting, You are God.

You turn man to destruction,

And say, "Return, O children of men."

For a thousand years in Your sight

Are like yesterday when it is past,

And like a watch in the night.

You carry them away like a flood;

They are like a sleep.

In the morning they are like grass which grows up:

In the morning it flourishes and grows up;

In the evening it is cut down and withers.

For we have been consumed by Your anger,

And by Your wrath we are terrified.

'A Prayer of Moses the Man of God'

You have set our iniquities before You,

Our secret sins in the light of Your countenance.

For all our days have passed away in Your wrath;

We finish our years like a sigh.

The days of our lives are seventy years;

And if by reason of strength they are eighty years,

Yet their boast is only labour and sorrow;

For it is soon cut off, and we fly away.

Who knows the power of Your anger?

For as the fear of You, so is Your wrath.

So teach us to number our days,

That we may gain a heart of wisdom.

Return, O Lord!

How long?

And have compassion on Your servants.

Oh, satisfy us early with Your mercy,

That we may rejoice and be glad all our days!

Make us glad according to the days in which You have afflicted us,

The years in which we have seen evil.

Let Your work appear to Your servants,

And Your glory to their children.

And let the beauty of the Lord our God be upon us,

And establish the work of our hands for us;

Yes, establish the work of our hands.

Promise Two:
A LAND OF THEIR OWN

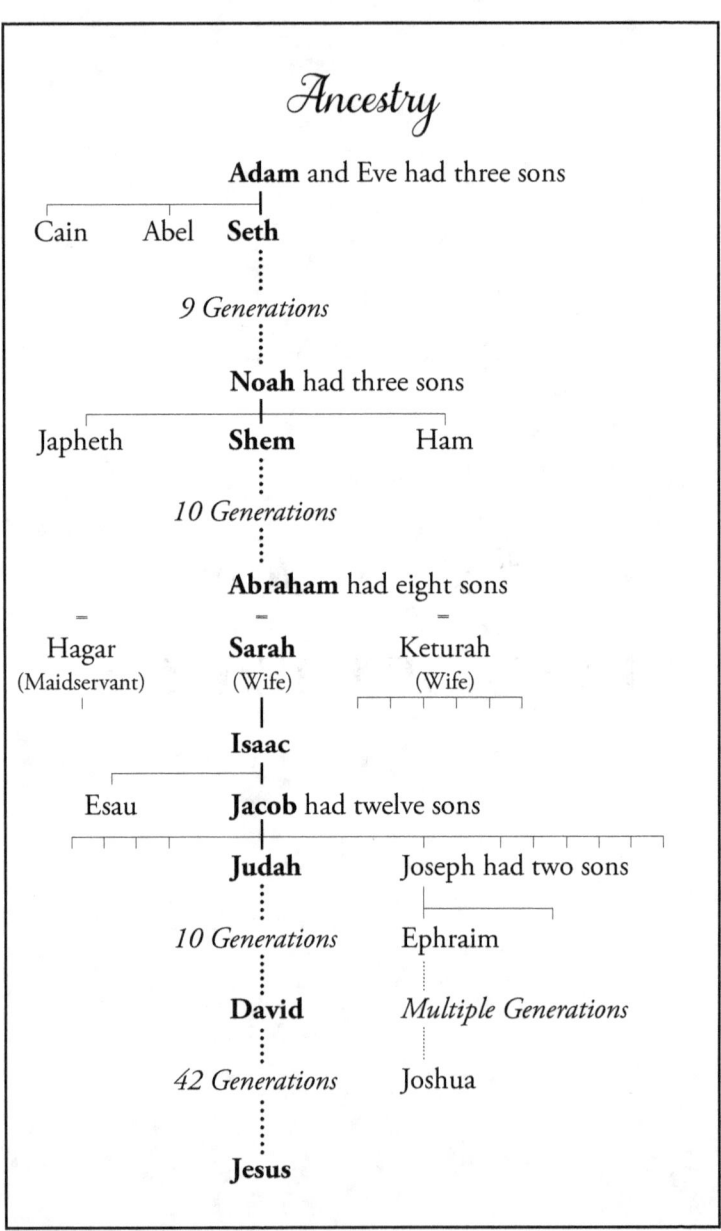

The Soldier of the Lord

*Now Joshua the son of Nun was full of the spirit of wisdom,
for Moses had laid his hands on him;
so the children of Israel heeded him,
and did as the Lord had commanded Moses.*

Deuteronomy 34:9

The Lord had inaugurated Joshua as the anointed leader of the children of Israel. He had been silently trained from his younger years to lead this people in the final conquest of the promised land. Joshua was the son of Nun, of the tribe of Ephraim, one of Joseph's sons. We first read about Joshua when Moses called him to lead the attack against the Amalekites not long after they had crossed the Red Sea, and many other times followed.

- Joshua led the assault on the Amalekites.
  Exodus 17:9
- Joshua accompanied Moses up Mount Sinai.
  Exodus 24:9–18
- Joshua remarked about the noise from the camp.
  Exodus 32:17

- Joshua stayed in the Tabernacle.
  Exodus 33:11
- Joshua questioned those who prophesied.
  Numbers 11:28
- Joshua was one of the twelve spies.
  Numbers 13:8
- Joshua encouraged the assault to proceed.
  Numbers 14:6–10
- Joshua and Caleb enter the promised land.
  Numbers 14:30
- Joshua and Caleb were exempt from the plague.
  Numbers 14:38
- Joshua and Caleb reprieved in the second census.
  Numbers 26:65
- Joshua was blessed by Moses for leadership.
  Numbers 27:18
- Joshua and Caleb fully followed the Lord.
  Numbers 32:12
- Joshua was responsible for tribe participation.
  Numbers 32:28
- Joshua is in charge of land distribution.
  Numbers 34:17
- Joshua is a reason for Israel to inherit.
  Deuteronomy 1:38.

Unbeknown to Joshua, God had continually trained him to be Moses' successor. Only Joshua, along with Caleb, out of millions, God acknowledged had fully followed the Lord. The time was right and the Lord spoke to Joshua and said:

> *"Moses My servant is dead.*
> *Arise, go over this Jordan,*
> *you and all this people,*
> *to the land which I am giving*
> *to the children of Israel."*

Joshua 1:2

The Lord outlined to Joshua what He had ordained. Everywhere they travelled was theirs, as no man shall be able to stand before him all the days of his life. I will be with you and not forsake you, so be strong and of good courage, be courageous. Always observe all the law and the commandments set down by Moses, so that you will prosper wherever you go. To make sure that the Book of the Law did not depart from his mouth, to meditate on it day and night, and to observe all that is written in it. Then finally the Lord said:

> *"Have I not commanded you?*
> *Be strong and of good courage;*
> *do not be afraid, nor be dismayed,*
> *for the Lord your God is with you*
> *wherever you go."*

Joshua 1:9

The time was right for the conquest of the promised land to continue. Reuben, Gad, and half the tribe of Manasseh had already taken possession of their inheritance, so Joshua reminded them of the promise they had agreed to with Moses and the Lord before Moses was called to be with his ancestors. The two tribes and half the tribe of Manasseh responded to Joshua that they would be faithful to their covenant previously agreed to. As this was completed, Joshua set the plan of the Lord in place, and the children of Israel eagerly awaited the next move.

The question that has surfaced is why the tribes of Reuben, Gad and half the tribe of Manasseh, were able to inherit the land where they were? The defeat of Sihon (Numbers 21:21–32; Deuteronomy 2:26–37; Judges 11:19–22, 6:3–5), established a foothold at the doorstep of Canaan, and control over a portion of the King's Highway finding land suitable for the tribes of Reuben and Gad in the process (Numbers 32:1–5, 32:33–36; Joshua 13:15–23). As they continued north and defeated Og king of Bashan at Edrie (Numbers 21:33–35; Deuteronomy 3:1–11), Moses assured Israel's influence in northern Transjordan.

Moses allowed part of the tribe of Manasseh to settle in Basham (Numbers 32:33, 32:40–42; Joshua 13:29–31). Recognising the strategic value of the Jordan Valley, Moses placed the tribe of Gad there (Numbers 32:33–36; Joshua 13:24–28). Returning to the Plains of Moab opposite Jericho, having secured the Transjordan, Moses now prepared the sons of Israel to move across the Jordan River into the long-awaited promised land. For the people of Israel, this was an in-between where they would not necessarily forget their dependence on

God (Deuteronomy 11:13–17; Proverbs 30:7–9), as this was a place specially prepared for them. Deuteronomy 32:8

Joshua was strategic in all his planning as he relied on guidance from the Lord. Joshua chose two men to leave Acacia Grove and secretly spy out the land, especially Jericho. The two spies were faithful in what Joshua had asked them to accomplish. They eventually stayed in the house of a harlot named Rahab. As they mingled with the guests, they were able to glean much information about the land from the travellers who lodged there. This was exactly what they required.

As Rahab was not a lady of the night, but the temple high priestess in Baal worship, she represented Asherah, Baal's consort. Baal worship was associated with the fertility of the land, and the people were taught that when Baal and Asherah were intimate with each other, the outcome was fertility for their land. As the priests and consorts imitated the gods and consented to sexual love, the land was fertilised. This was Rahab, and as she also owned an establishment for travellers to stay in, was the ideal place to socialise. Because she was the high priestess, she was held in high regard and her word would not have been doubted or questioned.

The two spies had not blended in as hoped, as the king of Jericho was told of their presence. When he sent word to Rahab to, *"Bring out the men who have come to you, who have entered your house, for they have come to search out all the country,"* this confirmed her thoughts and she took evasive action. The

Lord had brought the two spies under the protection of the one person in all Jericho who believed in Him.

When the two spies returned to Joshua, they told him all they had seen and heard. But there was something Joshua had not expected. The two spies had made a covenant with the high priestess Rahab for her protection and her family. How Baal worship had impacted Israel in the preceding days, and his two spies had made a pact with the high priestess, could have left Joshua wondering until they explained what had transpired.

Rahab understood and recognised why they were there, so she had perverted the king's messengers to provide protection by hiding them on her roof, then letting them down through the window in the side of the wall where her home was situated. Rules governed Rahab and her family who were sworn to secrecy. Not carrying out what had been agreed to, would dissolve the covenant and the two spies would be blameless. She had shown faith to carry out all they had said, by tying a scarlet cord in her window for them to recognise when the assault was over. Then the two men said to Joshua:

> *"Truly the Lord has delivered*
> *all the land into our hands,*
> *for indeed all the inhabitants*
> *of the country are fainthearted*
> *because of us."*

Joshua 2:24

The time had arrived to venture forward, so the children of Israel set out from Acacia Grove and camped at the Jordan River for three days. Joshua sent the officers through the Israelite camp to instruct them on the procedure that the Lord had put in place. When they saw the Ark of the Covenant of the Lord your God, the priests, and the Levites bearing it, then they were to follow but to leave just under a kilometre distance. This was set in place to show them the way, as none had been this way before.

The question could be asked as to why the pillar of cloud and fire was not leading them? Very little has been mentioned about these manifestations, apart from them gathering over the Tabernacle to show the presence of the Lord. At some time, it ceased, but when the most likely time was, we are not told. What we are told is, *"Be strong and of good courage; do not be afraid, nor dismayed, for the Lord your God is with you wherever you go"* (Joshua 1:9) It appeared that God assured Joshua He would be with Him, so all the others would benefit from Joshua being blessed by God. Just as God had parted the Red Sea for their ancestors, God was about to replicate the same procedure for the new generation of Israelites to witness.

In Joshua, we read, *"When you see the ark of the covenant of the Lord your God, and the priests, the Levites, bearing it, then you shall set out from your place and go after it"* (Joshua 3:3). They were following the Ark of the Covenant, not a cloud, pillars or a manifestation. Joshua told the people, *"As soon as the souls of the feet of the priests who bear the ark of the Lord rest in the waters of Jordan, the waters will be cut off. Then the priests who bore the ark of the covenant of the Lord, stood firm on dry ground, until all the people had crossed completely over the Jordan"* (Joshua 3:13a, 17). The Lord had promised to bring these people safely to the Promised Land, the land promised to Abram, as He provided protection, provision, and presence, as the Lord was true to His word.

Just as the clouds or pillars had ceased, so too had the manna. I guess forty years of this God-given food had proved enough. After they had crossed over the Jordan River and camped in Gilgal, we read the following. *"Now the children of Israel camped in Gilgal, and kept the Passover on the fourteenth day of the month at twilight on the plains of Jericho. And they ate of the produce of the land on the day after the Passover, unleavened bread and parched grain, on the very same day. Then the manna ceased on the day after they had eaten the produce of the land"* (Joshua 5:10–12a). This was the beginning of the Feasts of Israel, the Passover, the Feast of Unleavened Bread, and the Feast of First Fruits.

Joshua was about to experience his own encounter with the Lord. As Joshua was near Jericho, his eyes saw a Man who stood opposite him with His sword drawn in His hand. Joshua went near and asked if the Man was for them or against them? The Man replied, *"No, but as Commander of the Army of the Lord I have now come."* Joshua realised he was in the presence of the Lord and fell to the ground and worshipped, but the Man replied, *"Take your sandals off your foot, for the place where you stand is holy,"* and Joshua did so. Joshua 5:13-15

This private encounter with heaven preceded Joshua's public role at Jericho as he discovered that there was a Commander, mightier than he, who stood ready to lead the nation in conquest. When Joshua was asked to remove his sandals, this was a sign of humility and respect which he readily complied with, just as his predecessor had done at the burning unconsumed bush. When the Man referred to His being the *Commander of the Army of the Lord*, this was an indication that He led the innumerable heavenly bodies, which God had created. As God is referred to as the *'Lord of Hosts'*, He is not only the Lord of the armies of Israel but also has great spiritual armies at His command.

The Lord had assured Joshua, that even though the city of Jericho appeared to be impregnable, the king and the mighty men of valour were delivered into the hands of the Israelites. The Lord outlined specific instructions which Joshua and the children of Israel were to strictly obey. Seven priests who held seven trumpets of rams' horns were to walk before the Ark of the Lord followed by all the men of war, once around the city for six days, then they would return to camp.

The seventh day was different. Those who participated were to march around the city seven times exactly as had been completed in the preceding six days but when the priests blew the trumpets, Joshua gave the command and said to all the people, *"Shout, for the Lord has given you the city."* The people gave a great shout, and the wall fell down flat, so the people went up into the city, every man straight before him, and they took the city.

It should be noted that much teaching over the years has taught that the walls of Jericho, plural fell down flat, but the Bible clearly states that the wall fell down flat, indicating that only one wall fell. The question to be asked is, "Does this matter?" Well, it certainly mattered to Rahab and her family who were protected safely in her home in one of the walls. If all four walls had fallen, she and her family would have been killed, but as it was probably only the front wall that fell, she and her family were saved, as the spies had covenanted with her would happen.

Joshua remembered the conversation he had with the two spies regarding Rahab and her family. He said to the two men who had spied out the country,

> *"Go into the harlot's house,*
>
> *and from there bring out the woman*
>
> *and all that she has, as you swore to her."*
>
> Joshua 6:22

The young men rescued Rahab, her father, her mother, her brothers, and all that they had, then left them outside the camp of Israel (Joshua 6:23). The silver and gold, the vessels of bronze and iron were put into the treasury of the house of the Lord, the rest of the city was destroyed by fire. Nothing was to be personally taken. While Joshua spared Rahab and her father's household, Joshua cursed the city ruins never to be built again and if anyone did, their sons would die. The reason Joshua cursed the ruins of Jericho, this was the first of many conquests to the Lord, but as this was the first, it totally belonged to the Lord and was offered as a sacrifice.

The Soldier of the Lord

After the victory over Jericho, and its destruction, Joshua was eager to continue with their advancement, so he sent men to Ai to spy out the land. The men brought back a favourable report and were so confident in victory that they told Joshua he would only require a few, not the whole army to have victory. Joshua sent about three thousand men to Ai, but they fled before the men of Ai. About thirty-six were killed outright, the rest were struck down on the descent, so the people's hearts melted and they became very despondent.

The descent referred to meant the descent down the mountain range from Ai to Jericho. The mountain range was required to be negotiated to get to Ai, some twenty kilometres away and had an elevation of eighty hundred and twenty meters above sea level as Jericho was two hundred and seventy-six meters below sea level. A very steep mountainous path was one to be navigated by those who would travel or invade.

What had transpired was deflating for Joshua as he was well aware of the promises given to him previously about the presence of God protecting them, as He would be their constant companion. Joshua brought his grievance to the Lord, as he was prepared to stay on the other side of Jordan, not subject to annihilation little by little. Joshua had no words for the Israelites, but the Lord replied:

"Israel has sinned, and they have
even taken some of the accursed things,
and have both stolen and deceived;

> *and they have also put it*
> *among their own stuff."*
>
> Joshua 7:11

Joshua was about to learn that the sin of one person was borne by the whole nation. Through God's process, Achan was singled out as the one who had transgressed what God had commanded. Joshua brought to mind what God had said.

> *"And you, by all means*
> *abstain from the accursed things,*
> *lest you become accursed*
> *when you take of the accursed things,*
> *and make the camp of Israel a curse,*
> *and trouble it."*
>
> Joshua 6:18

Joshua questioned Achan as to the sin he had committed, and Achan confessed that he had sinned by converting, and then stealing what belonged rightly to the Lord. Joshua sent messengers to Achan's tent and retrieved the Babylonian garment, two hundred shekels of silver, and a wedge of gold weighing fifty shekels, and in front of the children of Israel, laid them before the Lord. Joshua took Achan, along with his family, his tent and all that he had to the Valley of Achor, where they were stoned and everything destroyed and burned. *"So the Lord turned from the fierceness of His anger."* Joshua 7:26b

The Lord assured Joshua that because the sin against Him had been rectified, He would protect and guide Joshua. The Lord also told Joshua that He was going to do the same to Ai as with Jericho, with one exception, the spoils and the cattle would be for themselves. As Joshua was confident that the Lord was with them, plans were again made to conquer this city and a different strategy was put in place.

Joshua chose thirty thousand mighty men of valour and sent them away at night to camp behind the city of Ai to wait in ambush, but to watch for his signal to attack and set the city of Ai alight so that it would burn. The thirty thousand went and stayed between Bethel and Ai on the west side, and as they left, Joshua re-joined the others and waited until morning.

Joshua rose early and along with the elders and all the people of war who were with him drew near and camped in a valley on the north side of Ai. Joshua took about five thousand men and placed them also on the west side of the city as an ambush. When all the people, all the army that was on the north of the city, and the rear guard on the west were in place, Joshua went into the valley during the night.

When the king saw Joshua and his army, he called all his troops to assemble and together they went out to do battle. As they were going out, Joshua and those with him fled as before, so all the army of Ai went after them. The Lord commanded

Joshua to stretch out the spear that was in his hand toward Ai. When those who were hiding in ambush saw the signal, they came up from behind the city and set the city alight, as there was no one left to protect the city and its occupants.

As the men of Ai saw the smoke of their city as it rose into the heavens, they fled from Joshua, but the ambush of the other fighting men of Israel emerged, who utterly destroyed all the fighting men and inhabitants of Ai. Joshua told the Israelites to take for themselves all the cattle and spoil as they required. So, the Lord brought victory to the children of Israel in the conquest of the land He had sworn to Abram as an inheritance.

Joshua remembered the command of the Lord that he was not to let the law of the Lord depart from his mouth, to meditate on it day and night, and to observe all according to what was written in it (Joshua 1:8). The time was right to again renew the covenant between God and the children of Israel, so Joshua built an altar to the Lord God in Mount Ebal, and in the presence of the children of Israel, wrote on the stones a copy of the law of Moses.

All of Israel along with their elders, officers, and judges, stood on either side of the Ark of the Covenant before the priests and the Levites who bore the Ark. Half were in front of Mount Gerizim and the other half in front of Mount Ebal. Joshua read all the words of the law, the blessings and cursing, according to what was written in the book, so all the people gathered could be blessed.

The Soldier of the Lord

> *"There was not a word of all that Moses*
> *had commanded which Joshua did not read*
> *before all the assembly of Israel,*
> *with the women, the little ones,*
> *and the strangers who were living among them."*
>
> Joshua 8:35

The Gibeonites had heard how the children of Israel were conquering their land, and they were seriously open to attack. The Hittites, Amorites, Canaanites, Perizzites, Hivites and Jebusites, allied to fight Joshua and the children of Israel, so a delegation of the Gibeonites met with the men of Israel and wanted to make a covenant with Israel, but they did not reveal they were neighbours. With all that the men said, no one sought counsel from the Lord, so Joshua and the Israelites were deceived.

When the truth finally surfaced, Joshua called them to himself and said:

> *"You are cursed, and none of you*
> *shall be freed from being slaves,*
> *woodcutters, and water carriers*
> *for the house of my God."*
>
> Joshua 9:23

The Gibeonites comprised people from Gibeon, Chephirah, Beeroth, and Kirjath Jearim. They confessed to Joshua their intentions for protecting their lives and told Joshua to do with them as he saw fit. While this contravened what the Lord had ordained, the people were delivered out of the hands of the children of Israel, and they did not kill them.

With the defeat of Jericho, Ai and the surrender of Gibeon and its confederated cities, the Israelites were driving a wedge between north and south. Little by little they were possessing the land. As Gibeon had surrendered to Joshua rather than fight, their desertion enraged the king of Jerusalem, who formed a confederacy with four of the neighbouring kings to attack Gibeon, who joined forces and attacked Gibeon.

Because they had covenanted with the children of Israel, the Gibeonites sent messengers to Joshua for help. Joshua was told by the Lord that they would have victory over those who had formed the confederacy, so Joshua gathered his troops and having marched all night came suddenly upon them at Gilgal. They slaughtered many and the rest fled, but as those who fled went down the descent of Beth Horon, the Lord sent great hail stones to rain on them and they died. Those who died from the hailstones were more than the children of Israel who had been killed with the sword.

The battle continued to rage with the Amorites, and as time was of the essence, Joshua prayed directly to the sun and the moon and his prayer was heard, by the command of God. Joshua prayed:

The Soldier of the Lord

> *"Sun, stand still over Gibeon;*
>
> *and moon, in the Valley of Aijalon."*
>
> *So the sun stood still, and the moon stopped,*
>
> *till the people had revenge upon the enemies.*
>
> Joshua 10:12b–13

This great miracle was the result of God's sovereign power in response to Joshua's authority in prayer. He spoke directly to the sun and moon, who obeyed God's command, and the sunset was delayed which enabled Israel to have revenge upon their enemies. Nothing like this had ever happened in the past, and nothing like this has happened since. Joshua continued his conquest of the southland, by defeating all those from Makkedah to Libnah, Lachish, Gezer, Eglon, Hebron, Debir, Kadesh-Barnea, Goshen, Gaza and the surrounding country.

> *"All these kings and their land*
>
> *Joshua took at one time,*
>
> *because the Lord God of Israel fought for Israel.*
>
> *Then Joshua returned,*
>
> *and all Israel with him to the camp at Gilgal."*
>
> Joshua 10:42–43

The kings of the north were fearful that Israel would attack them, so they formed together to fight Israel, but the Lord assured Joshua that they also would be delivered into their hands.

The Path of Life

So the Northern Campaign began as the Lord went before Israel to deliver all the land promised to Abram was delivered to them along with the cattle and spoils, and then they returned victoriously to Gilgal.

Joshua had patiently conquered much of the promised land, but he was old, and advanced in years. The Lord told Joshua that He would drive out the remaining inhabitants, but he was by faith to divide the land between the twelve tribes of Israel. Ephraim and Manasseh were allotted the portions due to Joseph, while the Levites received nothing as they were supported by all the tribes. Joshua 13:1

In all that had happened in the intervening years since the spies were originally sent into the promised land by Moses, Joshua and Caleb were the oldest. Caleb was just over forty years of age when selected as one of the original twelve spies, and Joshua was in his late forties. Now at the age of eighty-five, Caleb once more talked to Joshua about those past times and a land where his foot had touched that was not yet claimed, so Joshua allotted the land of Hebron to Caleb because he had wholly followed the Lord God of Israel. Joshua 14:6–15

Joshua continued to divide the land by casting lots to Judah, Ephraim and West Manasseh. Before any more division of land was carried out, Joshua and the whole congregation of the children of Israel gathered at Shiloh, and set up the Tabernacle of Meeting, and the land was subdued before them (Joshua 18:1). But seven tribes had not received their inheritance. Joshua rebuked these tribes and suggested the reason was because of complacency and laziness. Joshua proposed that three men from each of the seven tribes survey the remaining land, write a description of it, and divide the land into seven parts.

As the land division was carried out, Joshua continued and allotted each tribe their portion. The tribes involved were Benjamin, Simeon, Zebulun, Issachar, Asher, Naphtali and Dan. Not until all the tribes had received their portions did Joshua choose his inheritance and final resting place. Joshua chose Timnath Serah which was connected with the location where Joshua had commanded the sun and moon to stand still. Joshua 19:50

Joshua also set up cities of refuge where offenders from other places could find a safe place to live. Laws were also in place for those who chose to pursue this avenue. The Levites inquired about their inheritance and Joshua granted them to live and be supported by all the other tribes of Israel, as the Lord was their inheritance and to serve Him throughout the combined assembly. The Lord had fulfilled two of the three promises he had given to Abram as we read:

"So the Lord gave to Israel all the land
of which He had sworn to give their fathers,
and they took possession of it and dwelt in it."
Joshua 21:43

The children of Israel had learned many lessons as they learnt and travelled with both Moses and Joshua.

- God is faithful to the obedient.
- God fulfilled his promise of a land of their own.
- God had promised victory.
- God provided the promised rest.

Joshua 21:43–45

Joshua was very aware of the fighting force of Reuben, Gad and half the tribe of Manasseh, who had stayed true to their covenant with Moses and then Joshua. Joshua dismissed and discharged over forty thousand soldiers and were given his blessing to return to their families who had waited for at least seven to fourteen years for their return. Joshua 22:1–9

Much time had passed after the Lord had given rest to Israel. Joshua was well advanced in years so he called the children of Israel together for his two final messages. The first was addressed to the leaders, and the second to all the people. Joshua's message was about careful observance of God's Word, as three times he called them to obedience (Joshua 23:1–8, 9–13, 14–16). Each time he reminded them of what God had completed for them and urged them to be faithful.

Joshua was at the end of his life and like a father, he chose to leave the benefit of his wisdom to those who would follow in the path the Lord had set for them in the future. Israel was intended to be a blessing to the people around them, but because these nations resisted Israel as ambassadors of God's kingdom on earth, they were seen again as the enemy. Joshua continued to emphasized the need for obedience and to keep and advance their inheritance. As Joshua was about to obtain his eternal reward, his final messages was to provide Israel with his last will and testament for them to remember and apply.

Joshua called all the tribes to gather in Shechem which was located between Mount Ebal and Mount Gerizim. The situation provided a natural amphitheatre for a gathering, and because of its religious significance. God spoke through Joshua to all the people, reminding them of all that He had accomplished in the past. The main themes of the final message are reverence and respect toward the God who loves but is also just. God says seven times to serve, which meant to give allegiance exclusively to Him.

Joshua did not call the people to choose for themselves because he believed there were two options from God's perspective. By calling the people to choose, Joshua was able to affirm his loyalty to God and to urge a similar response from the people. The people's strong covenant response was undoubtedly sincere, however, for most, it did not develop as many forsook the Lord. Joshua assured the people that by not following the ways of obedience, would mean separation from the God who provided for them.

Joshua wrote what he had said in the Book of the Law, then on a large stone which he set up under the oak tree that was by the sanctuary of the Lord, as a reminder to all the people and future generations. After Joshua concluded his messages, he told all the people to depart, each to his inheritance.

Joshua was one hundred and ten when the Lord called him to his heavenly reward. Joshua was buried within the border of his earthly inheritance at Timnath Serah, which is in the mountains of Ephraim, on the north side of Mount Gaash. The book of Joshua concludes with the death and burial of three great men of Israel: Joshua, Joseph, and Eleazer, who had served Israel to gain her inheritance, and God's covenant had almost been fulfilled.

Promise Three:

A BLESSING TO OTHERS

Others Blessed

As Israel had become a great nation and growth continued, the third promise, *'to be a blessing'* was in place to be fulfilled. Teaching and obedience to what they had been taught, would bring a blessing to their families and their neighbours, to show the world how a God-centred life brought blessing.

When the Israelites were given their portion of land, they were supposed to drive out those who were antagonistic to their beliefs, but again, disobedience to the known will of God through compromise prevailed and this was not carried out. With compromise, they went against the promise, as the application of the teaching was the core ingredient for the success of the third promise given to Abram to be fulfilled.

While they had become a great nation and had their own land, the promise of being in charge to rule and bless others was never realised, even to this day as far as a true Jew is concerned. Many converted Jews have found the third promised blessing, and revel in the available power, but this is a spiritual power, not physical.

The world has yet to realise that *'Jesus is Lord'*, although many have experienced the blessing brought through the Jewish race, which was the Saviour of the world, Jesus Christ. This was the predestined will of Father God, which was distorted from the beginning.

When the Father did reveal His will through His Son, He was rejected by His own, as He did not fit the anticipated physical power they were expecting. Even the disciples, who were with Jesus throughout His ministry, asked Jesus at the last when He was going to restore the kingdom to Israel.

Simeon's prophesy over Jesus foretold of God's intention, but was again misunderstood. *"A Light to the Gentiles"*. One could imagine Mary and Joseph both wondering what the birth of their Son had to do with the Gentiles, the 'dogs' as they were commonly referred to by Jews.

When Caiaphas asked Jesus directly, *"Are You the Christ, the Son of the Blessed?"* Jesus said:

> *"I am.*
> *And you shall see the Son of Man*
> *sitting at the right of the Power,*
> *and coming with the clouds of heaven."*

Mark 14:61b–62

Although Jesus answered the priest's inquiry truthfully, they called it blasphemy. In Jesus' reply, He told them all that they were the judges now, but in the future, it would be He who would be judge over them.

The third promise has been fulfilled but not to the majority of the Jewish race who are still preparing for the One to free them from bondage. They are still anticipating His coming, carrying out the prescribed feasts and observing the holy days, but where is their remission for sin?

Remission for sin was in the shedding of blood through an animal sacrifice. How long has the practice of animal sacrifice been abandoned? Jesus said when addressing the Pharisees, *"You will die in your sins; for if you do not believe that I am He, you will die in your sins"* (John 8:24). If they didn't believe in Him, then they were lost for eternity.

So, what did the Jews implement to take the place of true atonement for sin? In Judaism, the Jews believe that God forgives, only when human beings sincerely seek to make amends in both mind and deed. On Yom Kippur, they say that repentance, prayer and charity will cancel whatever punishment they have earned through sin. Jesus said on another occasion, *"I am the way, the truth and the life, no one comes to the Father except through Me."* John 14:6

James, when writing to the twelve tribes of Israel that were scattered abroad said the following:

"Faith without works is dead."

James 2:17–26

Works will never get you into heaven, so what was James inferring when he said, *'without works'*? Our faith, which is the only way to please God, coupled with the works Jesus did, through His suffering and death, if not accepted, as James said *'is dead'*. Unless we accept what Jesus did for us through faith, our faith is dead.

Does this explain why so many Jews, although they live a wonderful life, are spiritually dead? This also applies to the vast majority of the world who have not recognised Jesus as their Lord and Saviour.

The time will come when all will be revealed and everyone without exception will bow down at the feet of Jesus and recognise His Lordship and Authority, but for many, when this time comes, it will be too late.

PART 2

Further INSIGHTS

The Journey

Moses and Joshua were both born into slavery but many years apart. Moses was well educated in all the Egyptian ways, originally from the tribe of Levi, but Joshua was a fighting man from the tribe of Ephraim. Moses enjoyed all the pleasures of Egyptian life for a time while Joshua was a slave and worked for the Egyptians making bricks for their buildings. When Moses fled Egypt and ended up in Midian, Joshua was only a young boy, who would have worked with his father, also a slave.

Moses had received many teachings in his life regarding the various gods. Jochebed instructed him in the one true God in his childhood years, then the pharaoh's daughter about all the Egyptian gods until he was forty years of age. Jethro, the priest of Midian, who accepted Baal worship, would have added more teaching over the next almost forty years. By the time Moses was about eighty years of age, he was a very mixed bag of deities. Only when God revealed Himself to Moses at the unconsumed burning bush, did Moses remember his previous teaching and his understanding that he would lead the people of Israel out of Egypt.

Moses went with his brother Aaron, and together they presented God's invitation to be free from the oppression of the Egyptians to the Hebrew elders. While many did not understand the consequences, they did accept Moses as their leader and would follow him, as he had the words of life and the promised land. They endured hardship and discouragement with their decision, but through perseverance, they left Egypt, as they followed the lead of Moses.

The Red Sea was their deliverance from oppression, which opened the way to the promised land and all this meant. They were taught the law and obedience with the consequences when they disobeyed. The building of the Tabernacle ushered in the Presence of Father God where they could worship Him. Previously, they only saw His Presence and Power, but now they were called to obediently walk where He led them without grumbling or complaining.

Our Journey

We are all born in bondage and slaves to sin, but at the right time, the Holy Spirit breaks into our life to invite us to follow Him in obedience as we did not choose Him, He chose us. Some embrace the calling without hesitancy, but others require persuasion as a time of persecution often presented itself, and one is concerned if this is what we want. When the decision is made, and we accept Jesus as the Lord and Saviour of our life, then by faith, we follow obediently the known will of God for us.

As we are the direct enemy of Satan, he would choose to bring us back under his control, but Father God, through the shed blood of His Son Jesus, and the power of the Holy Spirit, created a way for us to be released from the grip of the law, and embrace the potential plan God has ordained for us each, as we pass through the waters and emerge free to worship and serve the God who loves us.

We have passed from death to life, but only through obedience and remaining teachable to all that the Holy Spirit will impart to us, will remain free from the punishment and consequences of leaving or straying from the path. God gave us free will to choose and encouraged us to test all things, to be sure what is presented to us is the revealed will of God.

Many trials and temptations are encountered, which we were unaware of when the agreement to take on this journey was made, but one thing we have available to us that our predecessors the children of Israel did not have is Grace. Through what Jesus accomplished on the cross, and His resurrection from the dead, we have new life in Him, because of the Grace of Father God. James gave some words of wisdom when writing to the twelve tribes said:

"Count it all joy when you fall
into various trials,
knowing that the testing of your faith
produces patience."

James 1:2

Complete everything without grumbling or complaining as nothing was more abhorrent to God than the grumbling of the Israelites because He did not supply all they saw as their needs. In all their travelling and teaching, this was the most prevalent thing they never obtained or understood. Only a very select few out of millions, believed in the faith God had endowed on everyone.

Just as the Israelites had the Tabernacle, those of the called, have become, because of what Jesus accomplished on our behalf, priests, enabling us to go into the sanctuary and the very presence of Father God, where we can commune One with one, as led by the Spirit. We can go to the *'Incense Altar'* and render our prayers and petitions, to the Holy Spirit who then presents what we have said to Father God on our behalf. We boldly approach the throne of God because of the shed blood and washed clean by what Jesus did.

We have passed from death to life, Law to Grace, but remaining there depends on our willingness to obey. While Jesus blood covers most sin, it does not cover the sin of grieving the Holy Spirit, as we are told:

> "*Therefore I say to you,*
> *every sin and blasphemy will be forgiven men,*
> *but the blasphemy against the Spirit*
> *will not be forgiven men,*
> *in this age or in the age to come.*"
>
> Matthew 12:31, 32b

Further Insights: The Journey

As the Holy Spirit is our companion, we *'Tabernacle'* or dwell in the presence of Father God. We enter the dwelling place of God, through the *'Door'* which is Jesus that enabled us to go in and out and find pasture (John 10:9b). As God's presence was in the *'Pillars'* and the *'Ark of the Covenant'*, so we are invited, not compelled to follow the presence of Father God when He chooses or wills. We are not our own any more, as we have been brought with a price (1 Corinthians 6:19–20). While we are always free to choose for ourselves, because of what Jesus did, we choose to be His slaves, as we live each day in His care, as He, through the Holy Spirit, provides everything for us.

As hard times may be experienced, disobedience to the known will of God could take preference. If this occurred, we are encouraged to look, as the children of Israel did to the serpent on the uplifted pole, invited to look and live. Through the consequences of our sin, suffering and discomfort could continue for some to depths, only by the grace of God, they will be able to bear it, but God is faithful to the truly repentant sinner.

No matter how long or short our life, the option to enter the promised land will be presented to us, just as it was for the children of Israel. No one has any idea of what will transpire between our last conscience moment and the promised land. Jesus has forewarned us when He said:

> *"Enter by the narrow gate;*
> *for wide is the gate and broad is the way*
> *that leads to destruction,*

> *and there are many who find it.*
> *Because narrow is the gate*
> *and difficult is the way which leads to life,*
> *and there are few who find it."*
>
> Matthew 7:13–14

David when writing one of his psalms said:

> *"Yea, though I walk through the valley*
> *of the shadow of death, I will fear no evil;*
> *For You are with me;*
> *Your rod and Your staff, they protect me."*
>
> Psalm 23:4

Many may think the first verse represents the narrow door as us being presented with the invitation to accept Jesus as our Lord and Saviour, and rightly so. But what about when we pass from this life to the next, we need to remember that death is only a shadow, when we are in the presence of Jesus, for there is nothing to fear. How many times did Jesus say to His disciples, *"Fear not!"*

The whole journey of the Israelites can be seen as a foreshadowing of the life we are called to live as part of 'the called'. While we believe and remain in the arms of Jesus, there is always a choice. Faithful in all things, not grumbling or complaining, but accepting the Grace of God to cover all of life's situations, including our time to meet Him, we will be able to agree with Paul when writing his first letter to the Corinthians:

> *"O Death, where is your sting?*
> *O Hades, where is your victory?"*

1 Cor 15:55

The Passover

Roast one-year-old unblemished lamb, bitter herbs, and unleavened bread! What sort of evening meal is that? Besides, we need to be fully dressed as if we were about to travel. What does Moses think he is doing? The bread has always been made with some leaven. How much disruption and inconvenience has he brought to our way of life, as if we hadn't enough work to do without this imposition.

One could imagine this was the children of Israel as the future portrayed them as a people of grumblers and complainers. Moses had put in place what they were to accept in the future as the Passover when the Lord passed over all those homes that had blood on the doorposts and lintel.

The children of Israel did not observe the Passover again for just over a year. One could imagine them thinking they would celebrate this occasion in the *'Promised Land'*, but as the days turned into months, which became years, this was not the case.

Moses had issued many other instructions to be meticulously carried out, as well as taking some of the blood from the slain lamb and with the use of hyssop, applying it to the door posts and lintel. Unleavened bread was to be eaten for seven days and only those who were circumcised could partake. This was to be remembered as the Lord's Day, by His strong hand He delivered Israel from bondage. Exodus 13:1–10

The Lord had, through Moses, put in place the first of what would become the seven feasts of Israel, although the Israelites did not recognise the feasts in other areas of their worship, Father God had ordained would become an everlasting memorial to Him.

The Seven Feasts of Israel are:

- The Feast of Passover.
- The Feast of Unleavened Bread.
- The Feast of Firstfruits.
- The Feast of Weeks.
- The Feast of Trumpets.
- Yom Kippur.
- The Feast of Tabernacles.

The Feast of Unleavened included a day of preparation for the Passover, Unleavened Bread and the Feast of Firstfruits when only unleavened bread was to be eaten for the entire seven days. When the Tabernacle was constructed and set up, and the Presence of God filled the Tabernacle, each main item represented one of the feasts, although the children of Israel were unaware.

Further Insights: The Passover

Just as the pillar of cloud and pillar of fire had ceased, so too had the manna. I guess forty years of this God-given food had proven enough. After they had crossed over the Jordan River and camped in Gilgal, we read the following. *"Now the children of Israel camped in Gilgal, and kept the Passover on the fourteenth day of the month at twilight on the plains of Jericho. And they ate of the produce of the land on the day after the Passover, unleavened bread and parched grain, on the very same day. Then the manna ceased on the day after they had eaten the produce of the land"* (Joshua 5:10–12a). This was the beginning of the Feasts of Israel, the Passover which included the Feast of Unleavened Bread, and the Feast of First Fruits.

As my thoughts once again went to the Hebrews and the first Passover, I thought of the first time a communion meal was recorded in the Bible.

"Melchizedek king of Salem
brought out bread and wine;
and was the priest of God Most High."

Genesis 14:18

Melchizedek was Jesus who had taken on the form of a priest when He was talking and blessing Abram as they shared bread and wine as the bread was broken and the wine was shared and drunk.

There was another time when Jesus shared the Passover Meal with His disciples, for He said:

> *"With fervent desire I have desired*
> *to eat this Passover with you before I suffer;*
> *for I say to you, I will no longer eat of it*
> *until it is fulfilled in the kingdom of God."*
>
> Luke 22:15

When the Passover meal had finished, one could imagine Jesus looked at the table in front of Him and focused on two objects that He could visually use. Jesus, throughout His ministry, related objects and places to those of the crowds to explain what He was teaching. This night was similar as He wanted to share intimate details of the foreseeable future which involved Him.

Two objects stood out as Jesus focused on the table in front of Him. The unleavened bread and the wine they had been partaking of. As Jesus took the bread, gave thanks, broke the bread and passed the broken bread to His disciples, He said the words:

> *"This is My body which is given for you,*
> *do this in remembrance of Me."*

Jesus then took the cup of wine and said:

Further Insights: The Passover

> *"This is the new covenant in My blood,
> which is shared for you."*
>
> Luke 22:19–20

As I thought about these two occasions, bread and wine were used but at the Passover Moses had instituted, nothing to drink was mentioned as part of the meal. I then asked the question, "What did they drink?" As I reread the passage of scripture all I could find was whole roast lamb, unleavened bread and bitter herbs. Strict guided lines had to be observed, but the question reoccurred over and over, "What did they drink?"

Celebrations in the past appeared to have wine as an accompaniment, and just taken as normal, but this occasion was not normal, in fact, it was anything but normal. I refocused on the question and thought, "Where was the wine?" I continued to look at the prepared table before me to discover the truth and as I did, I was prompted to clarify my last question. The answer lay in the question I was asking, so what was I asking?

As I pondered my dilemma, I remembered Paul when writing to the Ephesians about the *'Armour of God'* (Ephesians 6:14–18), and how he never included any protection for their back. This was a similar situation as Paul's readers knew the answer when Isaiah wrote about the fast God required, for he said that when they were doing what the Lord required:

> *"The glory of the Lord*
> *shall be your rear guard."*
>
> Isaiah 58:8b

David then went on to explain the glory of the Lord when he wrote:

> *"Surely good and mercy will follow me*
> *all the days of my life;*
> *and I will dwell in the house of the Lord*
> *forever."*
>
> Psalm 23:6

Was my situation any different? The answer wasn't in "What did they drink", or "Where was the wine" but the real question was, "Where was the blood?" Jesus had shared with His disciples that the wine represented His blood given for them. The blood in this case was on the doorposts and the lintel. The blood was a covering for all those inside the house as they were protected when the Angel passed over them. They weren't required to have a physical drink when they had a spiritual covering.

What this means for us is that we are covered by Jesus' holiness, Jesus righteousness, and Jesus purity. We are covered by Jesus' blood, shed for us on the cross which means that, if we are *'in Christ'* when God looks at us, He sees Jesus first. As Paul says:

> *"For you died,*
> *and your life is hidden with Christ in God."*
>
> Colossians 3:3

This now asked another question, "How does God cover us?" The Lord completely covers us when we trust and know without a doubt that He is our refuge, strength, promise keeper and protection.

Water Supplied

Moses, apart from Jesus who was gentle and lowly in heart (Matthew 11:29), was the meekest man that ever lived (Numbers 12:3), but failed in his strong point. His failure spoiled a wonderful type of Jesus Christ, who was not smitten, hit a second time, and by so doing dishonoured the Lord and lost him the privilege of entering the Promised Land.

Apart from Jesus who was gentle and lowly in heart (Matthew 11:29), was the meekest man that ever lived (Numbers 12:3), but failed in his strong point. His failure spoiled a wonderful type of Jesus Christ, who was not smitten, hit a second time, and by so doing dishonoured the Lord and lost him the privilege of entering the Promised Land.

The children of Israel complained about the lack of water twice on their journey to the promised land. The first was not long after they had left Egypt, passed through the Red Sea and were camped at Rephidim in Horeb near Sinai (Exodus 17:1–7). The striking of the rock occurred before they were turned back from entering the promised land (Numbers 33:14), which meant this was associated with the slaves that Moses had led out of bondage.

The second time was in their fortieth year at Kadesh, the camp before Mount Hor on the edge of Edom where Aaron died (Numbers 33:36–39). This was the new generation as their predecessors had all but died, as the Lord told them would happen. The older generation now would have been under twenty years of age when the first supply of water was given by the Lord as all the others would have no recollection, only oral teaching, as they had been born after the miracle of the water.

The words used for 'Rock' are different in the two accounts. In the first story, the Hebrew word 'TSUR' means sharpness whereas in the second story, the Hebrew word 'CELA' is used and meant elevation. A parallel can be drawn by the first referring to Jesus as He was smitten in the sharpness of the Cross, while the second portrayed Jesus in the resurrection, raised and lifted up. The resurrected Christ needed only to be spoken to, to give the living water and not to be smitten again. John 7:37–39

The rods were also different as in the first case the Lord said:

"Take in your hand your rod
with which you struck the river, and go.
Behold, I will stand before you there
on the rock in Horeb;
and you shall strike the rock,
and water will come out of it,
that the people may drink."

Exodus 17:5a–6

Further Insights: Water Supplied

This was the miracle-working rod Moses had used before Pharaoh. In the second story, we read that Moses and Aaron were in the Tabernacle of Meeting before the Lord, when instructions from the Lord were given.

> *"Take the rod; Speak to the rock*
> *before the eyes of the congregation,*
> *and it will bring out water for them,*
> *and give drink to the congregation and their animals."*
> *So Moses took the rod from before the Lord*
> *as He commanded him.*
>
> Numbers 20:8–9

While Moses waited inside the Tabernacle in the Holy Place, Aaron, because he was the priest, went into the Holy of Holies, lifted the lid of the *'Ark of the Covenant'*, and removed the rod which had previously been his, which was kept as a reminder against the rebels. The rod of Moses represented the Law under which Jesus was crucified, whereas the rod of Aaron represented the priestly office where the risen Christ makes intercession for us. In the first case Moses struck the rock at the Lord's command, whereas in the second, Moses struck the rock twice contrary to the command to speak only to the rock.

In the first striking of the rock, Moses did not rebuke the people, but in the second instance, he called them rebels. Perhaps the rod which was *'a remembrance against the rebels'*, suggested this in his thinking. Moses called the first place Massah and Meribah, meaning *temptation* and *strife*, but we are told that Moses only used the second word 'Meribah', because:

> *"The children of Israel contended with the Lord,*
> *and He was hallowed among them."*
>
> Numbers 20:13

The whole incident is about Jesus so His work and ministry for the salvation of the world would take place. The first story implies that through the death of Jesus, our sins would be covered for all who would drink freely of His life-giving water. This part of Jesus' life would be recorded by Isaiah when he wrote:

> *"But He was wounded for our transgressions,*
> *He was bruised for our iniquities;*
> *the chastisement for our peace was upon Him,*
> *and by His stripes we are healed."*
>
> Isaiah 53:5

The second incident refers to the fact that Jesus' sacrifice was only necessary once, never to be repeated. To again crucify the risen Lord, repeating the finished work of Jesus Christ, is to bring dishonour to His glorious victory on the Cross. The writer to the Hebrews gave us words applicable to these thoughts when he wrote:

Further Insights: Water Supplied

> *"For it impossible*
> *for those who were once enlightened,*
> *and have tasted the heavenly gift,*
> *and have been partakers of the Holy Spirit,*
> *and have tasted the good word of God*
> *and the powers of the age to come,*
> *if they fall away,*
> *to renew them again to repentance,*
> *since they crucify again for themselves*
> *the Son of God, and put Him to an open shame."*
>
> Hebrews 6:4–6

The resurrected Christ enabled the Holy Spirit to act as we only need to speak the word in faith. Moses referred to the people as rebels, but at the same time he himself was in rebellion against the word of the Lord and his sin cost him the promised land. How easy is it to condemn others and sin in doing so? Jesus knew this was part of man, inbreed into his thinking as He reminded His listeners that while they saw the splinter in the eye of others, the plank in their eye should be addressed. Matthew 7:1–5

Though Moses acted contrary to the mind of the Lord in striking the rock a second time, instead of speaking to the rock, the water was provided for the children of Israel. Grace reigns even where sin or disobedience takes place. We need to remain faithful to the known will of God, as we listen with understanding as to what He asks us to do.

Paul when writing to Timothy a second time shared with him the following verses.

> *"This is a faithful saying;*
> *For if we die with Him,*
> *we shall also live with Him.*
> *If we endure, we shall also reign with Him.*
> *If we deny Him, He also will deny us.*
> *If we are faithless,*
> *He remains faithful;*
> *He cannot deny Himself."*
>
> 2 Timothy 4:11–13

The Tabernacle

To discover the significance, we need to note the objects in the *Tabernacle and their purpose, then observe how the seven "I AM"* sayings of Jesus, in true context, line up with the items in the Tabernacle and draw a conclusion from it. The Tabernacle consisted of the following:

- The perimeter had a gate (veil) in it.
- The Brazen Altar.
- The Laver.
- The Doorway (veil) into the Holy Place.
- In the Holy Place were the Golden Candlesticks,
- The Table of Shewbread,
- The Golden Altar of Incense.
- The Veil separated the Holy Place and the Holy of Holies.
- In the Holy of Holies was the Ark of the Covenant which consisted of the Ark proper, the Mercy Seat, the Cherubim and the Shekinah.
- Inside the Ark of the Covenant were the two tablets (Ten Commandments), Aaron's rod and a golden pot containing the Manna.

Jesus in His earthly ministry, taught seven main character parts as to Him and His Father were the same. Let's list the seven *'I Am'* sayings of Jesus.

- *I Am the Good Shepherd.*   John 10:11
- *I Am the Resurrection and the Life.*   John 11:25–26
- *I Am the Door.*   John 10:9
- *I Am the Light of the World.*   John 8:12
- *I Am the Bread of Life.*   John 6:35
- *I Am the Vine.*   John 15:5
- *I Am the Way, the Truth and the Life.*   John 14:6

The Lord revealed Himself to Moses at the burning bush as *"I AM THAT I AM"*, and told Moses to tell the children of Israel that the *"I AM"* had sent him to deliver them, in this the Lord Jesus claimed to be the *'I AM'*.

The Lord had previously revealed Himself through the Old Testament in the seven following ways:

- Genesis 15:1   *I Am your shield and your exceeding great reward.*
- Genesis 17:1   *I Am the Almighty God.*
- Genesis 31:13   *I Am the God of Bethel.*
- Leviticus 20:8   *I Am the Lord which sanctified you.*
- Psalm 35:3   *I Am your Salvation.*

- Isaiah 43:15   *I Am the Lord your Holy One.*
- Isaiah 48:12   *I Am the First, I also am the Last.*

A Gate

A way of entering the Tabernacle Courtyard (Psalm 100:4). All who wished to enter had no option but to use the veil or gate as getting in some other way meant you needed to climb the wall or break it down. The gate wasn't only accessible to the believers and priests, anyone could enter, walk around inside see what was happening and then walk out again.

Jesus taught about finding the *'Narrow Gate'* (Matthew 7:13–14), as Jesus said there was a large gate (veil) and a small gate (veil, door). The entrance to the courtyard was broad compared to the entrance (door, veil) of the Holy Place. Many people can come into our church, look around and go back out, but how many find the narrow door to salvation?

The Brazen Altar

"I Am the Good Shepherd.
The good shepherd gives His life for the sheep."

John 10:11

On entering the courtyard, standing midway between the gate and the door of the Tabernacle is the Brazen Altar. The altar was made of wood from the acacia tree and overlaid with bronze. Four horns projected from the top four corners, where the animals to be sacrificed were bound. The purpose of the altar *"was to make reconciliation upon"* (Leviticus 8:15), between God and His sinful people.

The Lord represented Himself to us as a Shepherd in the following ways.

- The Good Shepherd   John 10:11
- The Great Shepherd   Hebrews 13:20
- The Chief Shepherd of the sheep 1 Peter 5:4

Jesus referred to His own redeemed people, as those whom God had given to Him, who have believed in Him. He is the Shepherd and Overseer of our souls (1 Peter 2:25), as those who have accepted or returned to Him can say with David, *"The Lord is my Shepherd, I shall not want"* (Psalm 23:1). Psalm 100:3 says *"We are His people, the sheep He tends."* Jesus tending His sheep not only meant to feed, but also to look after, take care of, and restore.

When Jesus said, *"I am the Good Shepherd"*, it was an application of Psalm 23 to Himself, a claim to be God. The Jews so understood, for they took up stones to stone Him because, as they said, *"You being a Man make yourself God"* (John 10:33).

Further Insights: The Tabernacle

Jesus as Lord is still working today as:

- Our Lord marks His sheep by giving them the Power of the Holy Spirit.
- Our Lord still seeks the lost.
- Our Lord still provides a home for His flock.
- Our Lord will separate the sheep from the goats on Judgement Day.
- The Chief Shepherd is coming again soon. (1 Peter 5:4)

The Brazen Altar represented Jesus:

The Brazen Altar	**The Cross**
The sacrifice was without blemish	Jesus
From either the herd or the flock	Is the Lamb of God
A male	Is a male
Without defect	Is sinless
Be accepted on their behalf	He died in our place
To make atonement for them	Is our way to have forgiveness of sin
Blood sacrifice. Leviticus 1:2–5	Was the blood sacrifice made for us

The Laver

"I Am the resurrection and the life.
He who believes in Me,
though he may die,
he shall live.
And whoever lives and believes in Me,
shall never die."

John 11:25–26a

This beautiful vessel stood midway between the Brazen Altar and the Door of the Tabernacle and consisted of two parts, the Laver and its foot, which was made of brazen mirrors which were given by *"the women assembling at the door of the Tabernacle"* (Exodus 38:8). The women gave this offering as the Laver may have served the double purpose of a basin for the priests washing and as a mirror for cleanliness. The priests were required to keep themselves and their garments spotlessly clean because the penalty for neglecting to wash was very severe. *"When they go into the Tabernacle of the congregation they shall wash with water that they die not."* Exodus 30:20–21

What Jesus did enables us to have new life in Him, just as the priests washed themselves to make them acceptable to enter the Holy Place, so by washing in the Blood of Jesus, we are cleansed from all unrighteousness (1 John 1:9), joint heirs with Christ Jesus. Romans 8:12–17. v17

Further Insights: The Tabernacle Chapter

The importance of water is reflected in the following scriptures.

- Represents Quietness and Assurance   Psalm 23:2
- Represents Righteousness   Isaiah 35:6
- Represents Truth   Isaiah 28:2
- Represents Doctrine   Deuteronomy 32:2
- Represents Salvation   Isaiah 55:1; John 4:10

The washing doubtless pointed to the Holiness of God, to the pollution of sin and to the purity of heart necessary in those who would render acceptable worship. If the neglect of washing hands and feet with water was punishable with death, how hateful must an impure heart be in the sight of Him who is of purer eyes than to behold iniquity? The priests were required to draw near to God, not only with clean hands and feet but with a pure heart. No worship rendered by anyone can be pleasing to God, the Holy One of Israel, with clean hands, if the heart be polluted.

Matthew recorded Jesus' teaching, *"Blessed are the pure in heart, for they shall see God"* (Matthew 5:8). What does this mean for us? What does God do with our sin?

- Isaiah 1:18   *He washes them as white as snow.*
- Isaiah 1:18   *He washes them to be as wool.*
- Psalm 85:2   *He covers them.*
- Psalm 103:12   *Remove them as far as the east is from the west.*

Washing with water is frequently mentioned in the New Testament (Ephesians 5:26; John 3:3–5; Hebrews 10:22), and in every instance, it is unmistakably evident that the cleansing of the soul from the defilement of sins is to be understood. We must never forget that it is the Holy Spirit who takes the things of Christ and shows them to us.

The *'Brazen Altar'* typically pointed to the atoning work of Christ and the *'Laver'* to the sanctifying work of the Holy Spirit. If the *'Brazen Altar'* shows us that the guilt of sin can be cancelled by the blood of Christ alone, the *'Laver'* no less significantly teaches that the defilement of sin can be washed away by no other agency than that of the Holy Spirit.

Jesus Provided the Doorway

Before the 'Door' is presented, there is something in-between that is required to be noted. I would share the following verses with you.

But Jesus kept silent.
And the high priest answered and said to Him,
"I put You under oath by the living God:
Tell us if You are the Christ, the Son of God!"
Jesus said to him, "It is as you have said.
Nevertheless, I say to you,
hereafter you will see the Son of Man

Further Insights: The Tabernacle

> *sitting at the right hand of the Power,*
> *and coming on the clouds of heaven."*
> *Then the high priest tore his clothes.*
>
> Matthew 26:63–65a

"*He who is the high priest among his brethren, on whose head the anointing oil was poured and who is consecrated to wear the garments, shall not uncover his head nor tear his clothes*" (Leviticus 21:10). It was a danger of the priesthood that they might incur ritual contamination too close to an important ceremony to be able to purify themselves again and preside over the ceremony.

The time was in the morning and the priest would be offering '*The Passover*' that afternoon. There would be no intervening sundown to give time for a return to purity. There was no other except the Spotless Lamb of God who takes away the sin of the world, our Great High Priest. "*We have such a High Priest, who is seated at the right hand of the throne of the Majesty in the heavens*" (Hebrews 8:1). Another two-scripture verse will help bring clarity.

> "*But one of the soldiers*
> *pierced His side with a spear,*
> *and immediately blood and water came out.*"
>
> John 19:34

The Path of Life

> *So when the centurion and those with him,*
> *who were guarding Jesus,*
> *saw the earthquake and the things that had happened,*
> *they feared greatly, saying,*
> *"Truly this was the Son of God!"*
>
> Matthew 27:54

The *'Brazen Altar'* had all to do with the shedding of blood to make atonement for sins. The *'Laver'* had all to do with cleansing. The High Priest was required to fulfil the law set in place before he was able to carry out the Sacrifice, enter the Holy place and then the Holy of Holies. Because the High Priest had torn his clothes, he was defiled. There was no one to carry out the sacrifice but no one else was needed, as Jesus had accomplished it all.

When Jesus died on the cross, as the sacrificial lamb, who bore our sins, when His side was pierced, out flowed blood and water. Jesus combined both elements in His body to be once and for all our Great High Priest the only 'Doorway' into the Holy Place and the Kingdom of heaven.

Further Insights: The Tabernacle

The Doorway

"I Am the Door.

If anyone enters by Me,

he will be saved,

and go in and out and find pasture"

John 10:9

There were two doors: an outer and an inner (Exodus 26:31–37). The *'Outer Door'* (first veil, Hebrews 9:2) had a foundation of the very finest pure white linen yarn, and the weft of the same material dyed blue, purple and scarlet. The beautiful door hanging was suspended from five golden pillars standing before the entrance of the Tabernacle.

The *'Inner door'* or second veil, (Hebrews 9:3), was not only resplendent like the outer door hanging with blue, purple, scarlet and fine white linen, but was adorned all over with lovely cherubim figures, its chief characteristic. This gorgeous curtain was suspended from four golden pillars standing before the entrance into the Holy of Holies.

The purpose of the *'Doorway'* was to provide an entrance through which any who would enter the Holy place must go as no other way is available or acceptable. The Lord Jesus here represents Himself as the *'Door'* into Salvation, the only Way. Salvation is not something we receive from Christ, but something we have in Him. To have Salvation we must be *"found in Him"* (Philippians 3:9), neither is their Salvation in any other (Acts 4:12). To be found in Him we must enter in, by an act of faith that is like crossing the threshold of a door. There is *"no condemnation to them that are in Christ Jesus"* (Romans 8:1), for *"If any man be in Christ, he is a new creature: old things are passed away; behold all things are become new."* 2 Corinthians 5:17

John, when writing to the Church at Philadelphia says, *"I have set before you an open door and no one can shut it"* (Revelation 3:8). John also wrote to the Church at Laodicea and said, *"Behold, I stand at the door and knock. If anyone hears My voice and opens the door, I will come in and dine with him, and he with Me"* (Revelation 3:20). Again John in Revelation 4:1, writes about a *'Door'* in Heaven, a door where the righteous enter, who have washed their robes and made them white in the *'Blood of the Lamb'*. Revelation 7:14

The question could be asked, "Will this Door always be open?" More than once the Lord warned us that the door would one day be shut that is, the day of Grace ends and Mercy's offer be closed. It was so in the Parable of the Ten Virgins for when the five foolish arrived it was too late as *"The door was shut"* (Matthew 25:12). One day the Master of the house will rise up and shut the door, and then it will be too late to knock and find an entrance.

Jesus came to give a full life to those who trust Him, a life abundant with joy. Jesus said:

- He is the only *Way* to God.
- His Word is the only *Truth*.
- Eternal *Life* can only be found in Him.

Jesus emphasized that no one can come to God any other way, as Jesus is the only way to God. The only way into the *Holy Place* and into the presence of God was through the *Door*. In John 14:6b Jesus said, *"No one comes to the Father except through me."* Jesus, our *Door*, takes us into the presence of God.

The Golden Candlesticks

"I Am the light of the world.

He who follows Me shall not walk in darkness,

but have the light of light."

John 8:12

This splendid lamp standing on the left-hand or south side of the Holy Place (Exodus 40:24), was made entirely of pure gold and was beaten, not cast in a mould, but formed by hand from one piece of material (Exodus 25:31). The base had an upright branch or stem which constituted the candlestick proper (Exodus 25:31–38), out of which came six branches like arms, three out of one side and three out of the other (v32). Both threes were parallel to each other as they all curved upwards to an equal level. The central branch was a little higher than the other six and was to burn continually (Leviticus 24:2). As there were no windows in the Tabernacle and the priests had duties to perform during the day in the Holy Place, it is accepted that the *Golden Candlestick* gave the only light to light the Holy Place.

Its purpose was to give a continuous light to the Holy Place. Jesus said, *"I am the light of the world. He who follows Me shall not walk in darkness, but have the light of life"* (John 8:12). Jesus explained how He was the light when He said, *"No one has seen God at any time. The only begotten Son, who is in the bosom of the Father, He has declared Him"* (John 1:18). Only in Jesus is God, Who is Light, known. Jesus is the only source of the knowledge of God as Jesus caused the blind to see when on the earth, so He opens the blind eyes of the heart of the natural man and shines in with the knowledge of Salvation.

As a light, He guides. John 8:32 says, *"And you shall know the truth and the truth will make you free."* Jesus also said, *"When He, the Spirit of truth has come, He will guide you into all truth"* (John 16:13). As the *Guide* of the child of God, He gives to all who believe and guides them into all truth.

On another occasion, Jesus said, *"As long as I am in the world, I Am the light of the world"* (John 9:5). The lights in the heavens all speak to us of Jesus as Jesus represented the Sun. The Church, having no light of its own, is like the Moon whose light is the reflection of the Sun. The Stars are like individual Christians (Daniel 12:3) each shining in their place. The Pillar of Fire (Exodus 13:21), is another picture of Jesus as the Light of Life guiding His people by the Holy Spirit through the darkness of this world.

Further Insights: The Tabernacle

John, when writing his epistle said, *"If we walk in the light as He is in the light, we have fellowship with one another, and the blood of Jesus Christ His Son cleanses us from sin"* (1 John 1:7). We need to exercise faith and yield obedience to the Lord Jesus along with the truth of His word and conviction of His Spirit. This is the obedience of Faith. If we do so, we shall never miss the Light on our path as we have the Light of Life.

As the Holy Place in the Tabernacle was illuminated by the sevenfold light of the candlestick, so the church, composed of genuine believers enlightened by the Holy Spirit, will triumph in heaven, that Great Temple, not made with hands, but a place of glorious light; and the light will never go out, as it will burn always; so there will be no night there; nor the sun, nor moon, nor stars will shine in that happy place, *"For the glory of God did lighten it, and the lamp thereof is the Lamb."* Revelation 21:23

The Table of Shewbread

"I am the bread of life.
He who comes to Me shall never hunger,
and he who believes in Me
shall never thirst."

John 6:35

The Table of Shewbread was a small table made of acacia wood and overlaid with pure gold. Its place was on the right side of the Holy Place. The priests baked the bread with fine flour and it remained on the table before the Lord for a week. Every Sabbath day the bread was renewed and only the priests could eat the bread as it could only be eaten in the Holy Place because it was Holy. The Shewbread was also called *"Presence Bread"* because it was in God's dwelling place and before the symbol of His presence, the veil only intervened.

The purpose of the *'Shewbread'*, ever lying on the table, was a constant reminder of God's goodness in providing for the nourishment of His people. Jesus referred to Himself as the *Bread of Life* which John recorded in his gospel. When John 6:31 to 63 is read, the following can be found.

- Verse 32   The true bread from heaven.
- Verse 33   The bread of God.
- Verse 35   The bread of life.
- Verse 48   The bread of life.
- Verse 51   The living bread.

The Lord was watching over the Israelites when He led them out into the Sinai wilderness. This desolate wasteland was devoid of enemies, but there was also very little food. The people grumbled and wanted to return to slavery as their attitude toward the Lord's provision was saddening because the Lord would not abandon them if only they would ask, but no, they grumbled. The Lord provided bread and meat for them and they didn't even have to work. For six days out of seven, Manna was supplied which reminded them, *"It is the Lord who provides."*

Just as the priests were able to take the bread and drink the wine so we too are to take and eat of Christ and know that it is good for our souls. We need to continually feast from His banqueting table taking what we need to satisfy our spiritual hunger. Unlike the priests, who had to wait for the end of the week, because of what Jesus did, we can march right in and ask for what we need at any time. Christ is the Head of the Church and we are the body of Christ.

The Golden Altar.

"I am the vine, you are the branches.
He who abides in Me, and I in him,
bears much fruit;
for without Me you can do nothing."

John 15:5

The golden altar sat in the centre, at the west end, in front of the curtain (veil) that separated the Holy Place and the Holy of Holies. The Lord commanded the priests to burn incense on the golden altar every morning and evening, as the incense was to be a continual pleasing aroma to the Lord throughout the day and night. Live coals were taken from the brazen altar and put upon the golden altar for burning the incense. The clouds of smoke full of perfume spread their fragrance all around, penetrating the veil and reaching even to the throne. The priest, while presenting this offering, was the people's intercessor with God, praying for them and asking Him to hear and answer their petitions.

The purpose of the incense was a symbol of the prayers and intercession of the people going up to God as a sweet fragrance. God wanted His dwelling to be a place where people could approach Him and pray to Him. Jesus, our Great High Priest, told us to ask for what we need (John 15:7), as the Lord is waiting to grant us our needs. The sweet fragrance of our prayers drifts up into heavenly places.

Most Holy Place

"I am the way, the truth, and the life.
No one comes to the Father
except through Me."

John 14:6

The Ark of the Covenant was the chief and most sacred of all the objects connected with the Tabernacle. Its pre-eminence is further indicated in it being the first object that God spoke to Moses about and commanded to be made (Exodus 25:10–22). It consisted of four distinct objects.

- The Ark itself,
- the Mercy Seat,
- the Cherubim,
- the Shekinah.

Further Insights: The Tabernacle

The Ark was made of acacia wood overlaid inside and out with pure gold. Inside the Ark were the two tables of stone on which the Ten Commandments were written, a golden pot containing Manna and Aaron's budding rod.

The purpose was the Lord's special dwelling place amid His people as it was also the place where the Lord showed Himself merciful in forgiving sin. The Lord Jesus not only claimed to be the *'Door'* into Salvation and Life but the *'Way'* upon which the believer entered when they crossed the threshold of the door. The *'Truth'* by which they are guided in the *'Way'* and the *'Life'* by which they are invigorated and maintained as they pursue their journey along the way that led to the Father.

As the *Ark of the Covenant* stood within the Holy of Holies, it was a type of Jesus. It was the symbolic *Throne of God* and reminds us that God is enthroned in Jesus. It is *'in Christ'* that He met the sinner, who, now that Jesus has died and the *Veil* has been torn, the *Blood* sprinkled on the *Mercy Seat*, is asked to draw near (Hebrews 10:22), to come boldly to the *Throne of Grace*, that he may obtain and find grace to help in time of need. Hebrews 4:16

The contents of the Ark of the Covenant were two tables of stone (Ten Commandments), the golden pot containing Manna (Exodus 16:33–34), and Aaron's budding rod (Numbers 17:10). The ark may be regarded as the Heart of Jesus, for it is written, *"Your law is within my heart."* Psalm 40:8

What is the significance of the two tables of stone? They remind us of Righteousness and Truth as the Manna spoke of Jesus as the Food for His people, He Himself claiming to be the *Bread* which came down from *Heaven* of which if a man eats he shall never die (John 6:50). The Rod reminds us of His *Authority* as the High Priest and the Fruitful Branch or New Life. Each of these is also a reminder of the sin of the people when placed into the Ark.

How can we now view John 14:6? I Am the *Way* (through the torn veil), the *Truth* (righteousness and truth found in the Ten Commandments) and the *Life* (Authority and fruitful new life), no one comes to the Father except through *Me* (Our Great High Priest). Jesus Christ is Himself the *Way*. He does not point out the *Way* as a teacher, nor show us the *Way* as our example because He is the *Way*. I must receive Him (John 1:12), and be found in Him (Philippians 3:9), or I shall miss the *Way*.

Conclusion

As each part has been mentioned, they all represented Jesus and what He taught. But there is one observation that could be easily overlooked and that is *'The Cross in the Tabernacle'*. If you draw a line from the Holy of Holies, through the Incense Altar to the Door, then a second line from the Golden Candlesticks to the Shewbread Table, which passes through the Incense Altar, a Cross is formed. The Tabernacle is all about Jesus and a foreshadowing of the future which was hidden from the children of Israel.

The Camp of Israel

The children of Israel had left Egypt in an orderly fashion. After they arrived at Mount Sinai, the Law given, the Tabernacle built and constructed, the Lord called for a census of all the Israelites. Once this was completed, Moses knew how many belonged to each of the twelve tribes, the Levites and the mixed multitude who accompanied them.

Every detail is by design, so what might be hidden behind the details of the Camp of Israel? The fulfilment of prophesy concerning Jesus and His work is recorded in the following verse:

> *"The volume of the Book is written of Me."*
>
> Psalm 40:7 and Hebrews 10:7.

The Levites were not numbered but were to look after the Tabernacle and camp around it. Numbers 1:50.

In the second chapter of Numbers, the designated campsites were laid out.

FOUR CAMPS

Judah	74,600	Ephraim	40,500
Issachar	54,400	Manasseh	32,200
Zebulun	57,400	Benjamin	35,400
Total:	186,400	*Total:*	108,100
Reuben	46,500	Dan	62,700
Simeon	59,300	Asher	41,500
Gad	45,650	Naphtali	53,400
Total:	151,450	*Total:*	157,600

TOTAL: 603,550

The Levites camped around the Tabernacle.

The Camp of Judah............ East of the Levites.
The Camp of Reuben......... South of the Levites.
The Camp of Ephraim....... West of the Levites.
The Camp of Dan.............. North of the Levites.

Strict obedience to God's instructions denies any other area.
Only the original directions are used.
Only the width of the Levites Camp is used.
Length is proportional to the population.

Further Insights: The Camp of Israel

Let's set the Tabernacle in place with the Levites camped around it.

Now each of the four Camps is ordered by God.
Note: North and South are twice as wide as East and West.

What do we see?

"A CROSS IN THE DESERT"

West

Ephraim	40,500
Benjamin	35,400
Manasseh	32,200
Total:	108,100

South

Reuben	46,500		**Levites**		Dan	62,700
Simeon	59,300		**Camp**		Asher	41,500
Gad	45,650				Naphtali	53,400
			around			
Total:	151,450		**Tabernacle**		Total:	157,600

North

Judah	74,600
Issachar	54,400
Zebulun	57,400
Total:	186,400

East

Midianites

The Lord had one last assignment for Moses to complete before he was gathered to his people. The Lord said:

> *"Take vengeance on the Midianites*
> *for the children of Israel."*
>
> Numbers 31:2a

This would have not been any surprise to Moses as he knew the hearts of the Midianites, because he had walked and seen the five cities and observed the religious practices and beliefs of the people. Baal worship was the core of their lifestyle, so different to the God he knew who led and guided him in his every action. For almost forty years he had lived with a Midian priest by the name of Jethro and his family. What he had taught and practised did not sit well with Moses, but he endured until God called him to fulfil his calling.

Just after the children of Israel had settled into Acacia Grove, adjacent to Jericho, some of the Israelites played the harlot in Moab when they joined with the women of Moab in the worship of Baal of Peor, which angered the Lord. Although many Israelites were killed for their actions, as they deliberately broke the commandments, the Lord required revenge for the dealings of Balaam when teaching the young women how to prostitute themselves with the men of Israel. Numbers 31:16

Phinehas, the son of Eleazer the priest, noticed an Israelite by the name of Zimri from the tribe of Simeon, take a Midianite woman whose name was Cozbi, the daughter of Zur, one of the five kings of Midian into his tent blatantly in front of the Israelites. Phinehas took a javelin, entered their tent where he plunged it through them both, and they died.

With all this in mind, Moses ordered the attack on the Midianites, and they killed all the fighting men, the five kings as well as Balaam. When I read these verses, I wondered what happened to Jethro and his family.

When Moses was forty and had just killed an Egyptian, he fled to Midian. It was here he defended the shepherdesses from the other shepherd bullies. Moses was invited to the home of Jethro, where he stayed for almost forty years.

Jethro was the priest of Midian and had seven daughters. He gave Zipporah to Moses who became his wife and they had two children. When Moses was confronted at the unconsumed burning bush about his calling, he and his family went to Egypt. Moses didn't relate his God-given calling to Jethro, but said he would go and see if his family was still alive. This could have been because Moses and Jethro did not agree on spiritual matters and worship practices.

Further Insights: Midianites

After the situation became tense in Egypt, Moses sent his wife and children back to Midian for safety reasons. One could imagine that Jethro was concerned when his daughter and two sons arrived home but no Moses. As Jethro asked the hard questions, Zipporah told her father the truth behind Moses' return to Egypt. When Moses was at Mount Sinai, Jethro brought his wife and sons back to meet him, as Jethro had heard all that the Lord had accomplished through Moses and the Israelites.

Jethro was a priest in Midian, where the culture embraced Baal worship. When Jethro talked with Moses, it appeared he had been converted from Baal worship to worshipping the God of Moses for he said to Moses:

> *"Blessed be the Lord,*
>
> *who has delivered you out of the hand of Pharaoh,*
>
> *and who has delivered the people*
>
> *from under the hand of the Egyptians.*
>
> *Now I know that the Lord is greater than all the gods;*
>
> *for in the very thing in which they behaved proudly,*
>
> *He was above them."*
>
> Exodus 18:10–11

Jethro was joined by Aaron the next day and all the elders of Israel when Jethro took a burnt offering and made sacrifices to offer before God. Aaron and the elders had witnessed first-hand the change that had taken place in Jethro so they all shared in eating bread together. By this act, Aaron and the elders conveyed to Jethro that he was accepted and part of their family. After some timely advice from Jethro to Moses about delegation, he bid farewell to Moses and returned to Midian. Exodus 18:27

Moses continued to do the revealed will of God, as he was given the Law on the two tablets but then smashed the tablets in a rage when he saw the children of Israel after they had accepted the commands of God and broken at least three within the first forty days, worshipping the golden calf.

Moses arranged for Bezalel, from the tribe of Judah and Aholiab from the tribe of Dan to take charge of building all the various parts of the Tabernacle. When everything was finished, Moses inspected to make sure what had been completed met God's specifications. When the Tabernacle was constructed, the presence of God filled the Tabernacle.

Moses was instructed to carry out a census, which allowed him to know how many people belonged to each of the twelve tribes and the Levites. God counselled Moses on how to set out the camp and where each tribe was to camp.

The second Passover feast was observed in the second year after they had left Egypt, as the previous year the Passover had been ignored. On the last day of the Feast, the cloud began to move which signalled to the Israelites, that they were to pack up and move.

Further Insights: Midianites

It is now we are introduced to another family member, a Kenite, the brother-in-law of Moses, who possibly arrived with Jethro, his father-in-law. Moses says to Hobob:

> *"We are setting out for the place*
> *of which the Lord said, 'I will give you.'*
> *Come with us, and we will treat you well;*
> *for the Lord has promised*
> *good things to Israel."*
>
> Numbers 10:29

Hobob had married another of the seven daughters and we are told he was a Kenite, who was descended from Cain, a cursed race of people. Did Hobob stay or did he go back to Midian to be with Jethro and the rest of the family? We read more of the conversation Moses had with Hobob.

> *"I will not go, but I will depart*
> *to my own land and to my relatives."*
> *So Moses said, "Please do not leave,*
> *inasmuch as you know how we are to camp*
> *in the wilderness, and you can be our eyes.*
> *And it shall be, that whatever good the Lord*
> *will do to us, the same we will do to you."*
>
> Numbers 10:30–32

From the arrival of Jethro and Hobob to the children of Israel moving after a prolonged stay at Mount Sinai, could have been a timespan of eighteen months. Hobob would have observed the golden calf worship, the giving of the commandments, the construction and building of the Tabernacle, the census, and the placement of the twelve tribes as they camped around the Tabernacle and the Levites.

When Moses ordered the slaughter of all the men of Midian, did this mean Jethro, his father-in-law and Hobob his brother-in-law? When the females and children were brought back captive, Moses was angry and had all the boys and those women who had been intimate with a male slaughtered as well. Did this include the family of Jethro, his daughters and their families?

The war the Lord had declared to Moses to carry out against the Midianites was not the normal understanding of complete annihilation, but a holy war of cleansing as the twelve thousand fighting men, a thousand from each tribe were led by Phinehas the son of Eleazar the priest. It would appear that anything and anyone who was associated with Baal worship was killed or destroyed. This is brought to light when the division of plunder was completed, as thirty-two thousand persons, and women who had not known a man intimately were counted. Numbers 31:35

The questions to be asked are, when Jethro returned to Midian, after so much opposition as a priest who had a complete turnaround in his worship practises, and understanding, from idol worship to the worship of the true God, did he find the way too hard and re-joined the children of Israel? And what of Hobob? Did he leave Moses to look after the encampments on his own, rather than a support and stay for him?

In the book of Judges, the following is recorded to shed a little light on what had happened previously.

> *"Now the children of the Kenite,*
> *Moses' brother-in-law,*
> *went up from the City of Palms*
> *with the children of Judah*
> *into the Wilderness of Judah,*
> *and dwelt among the people."*

Judges 1:16

The passage in Judges 1:16 showed that Hobab's descendants eventually did end up in the land of Canaan. The verse suggests that Hobab changed his mind and did go with Moses and Israel into Canaan, and the descendants of the Kenite, Moses' brother-in-law, went up with the people of Judah from the City of Palms, which was Jericho and its oasis, into the wilderness of Judah, which lies in the Negeb near Arad, and they went and settled with the people. As for Jethro and the rest of his family, we are not told.

Jericho and Beyond

In the time of Jesus, Jericho was beautiful in situation, a city of palm trees, and had become the priestly city where the religious leaders lived when not fulfilling their duties. Jerusalem, the city of history and religion, was the centre of privilege. It had been a long time since Joshua and the children of Israel fought the battle of Jericho.

Joshua and the Israelites had just witnessed the wall of the city of Jericho fall and had advanced to plunder the city to retrieve all for the Lord as He had commanded.

Joshua saw the two messengers who had made a covenant with Rahab and told them to rescue her household and their possessions. The two messengers looked at the remaining walls and saw the scarlet cord still in place as she had been instructed to do, so they knew exactly where to go and rescue her and her household.

When the spies told Rahab to do this, they possibly reflected on the time when their ancestors had left Egypt and were instructed to place blood on the doorposts and lintel for protection which avoided disaster. A scarlet cord would be representative of the blood and protected Rahab and her family as long as they stayed inside the home.

The two messengers found Rahab along with the other members of her family and took them to a safe place outside the camp of Israel. The scene must have been horrific as they witnessed everyone killed and all the treasure bought out and placed in the treasury which belonged to the Lord, then Jericho set ablaze. The children of Israel understood that the city had been declared as belonging to the Lord because He had said:

"Now the city shall be doomed by the Lord
to destruction, it and all who are in it.
Only Rahab the harlot shall live,
she and all who are with her in the house,
because she hid the messengers that were sent."

Joshua 6:17

The faith of Rahab had saved herself and those near and dear to her from utter destruction. It would have been an uneasy feeling for the high priestess of Baal to be among those who believed in the One true God. How would they react to them as they joined the camp? What would become of them now? Was it worth them betraying all their friends? As they watched, Joshua placed a curse on their beloved city, which now lay in ruins.

"Cursed be the man before the Lord
who raises up and builds this city, Jericho;

Further Insights: Jericho and Beyond

he shall lay its foundation with his firstborn,
and with his youngest he shall set up its gates."

Joshua 6:26

Joshua took these refugees and placed them in the care of those in the tribe of Judah where they would have been instructed in the ways of the Israelites. Acceptance of this new way of life was embraced because they were grateful for how they had been saved and given a new life as they didn't grumble or complain like some of the others.

Rahab had no idea when she protected the two messengers, that because she feared the God of the Israelites more than their gods, she was inducted into the plan of redemption, and would help to fulfil the third blessing, that the Israelites would be a blessing to others.

In time, Rahab fell in love with a Judean by the name of Salmon. During the conquest of the southland and the northern conquest, after Joshua had allotted to the twelve tribes their inheritance and settled into a life without fighting, Salmon and Rahab had been blessed, over time with three sons. The first was Elimelek, the second was unnamed, and the third was Boaz.

As a severe famine was upon the land of Judah, and in Bethlehem, Elimelek, Naomi and their two sons, Mahlon and Chilion packed up and dwelt in the country of Moab which had been allotted to the tribe of Reuben. Terah was the father of Abram and Nahor who had a son by the name of Lot, the distant ancestor, who had two sons Moab and Ben-Ammi, who established the tribes of the Moabites and the Ammonites.

Not long after the family had settled into this new lifestyle, Elimelek died. The two sons then took wives for themselves from the women of Moab, Orpah and Ruth, not from their tribe of Judah. After about ten years, both sons died and Naomi was left with two daughters-in-law.

Naomi thought it wise to return to Bethlehem, as she had heard that the Lord had visited His people by giving them bread. When she told Orpah and Ruth her intentions, Naomi bid them farewell, but while Orpah returned to her people, Ruth said:

> *"Entreat me not to leave you,*
> *or to turn back from following you;*
> *for wherever you go, I will go;*
> *and wherever you lodge, I will lodge;*
> *your people shall be my people,*
> *and your God, my God.*
> *Where you die, I will die,*
> *and there will I be buried.*
> *The Lord do so to me, and more also,*
> *if anything but death parts you and me."*
>
> Ruth 1:16–17

Further Insights: Jericho and Beyond

The youngest son of Salmon and Rahab, Boaz, had grown up but never married. As their son grew, he became wealthy and treated his workers with respect as he would greet them with:

> *"The Lord be with you!"*
>
> *And they answered him,*
>
> *"The Lord bless you!"*
>
> Ruth 2:4b

One day when Boaz was in the field, he talked with one of his servants who was in charge of the reapers, as he noticed a young girl gleaning the barley crop. Although she was a foreigner, she was able to glean as the law provided for such people. The law said:

> *"When you reap the harvest of your land,*
>
> *you shall not wholly reap the corners*
>
> *of your field when you reap,*
>
> *nor shall you gather any gleaning from your harvest.*
>
> *You shall leave them for the poor and for the stranger:*
>
> *I am the Lord your God."*
>
> Leviticus 23:22

Boaz found out her name was Ruth and a distant relative of his. He protected her by insisting she only glean in his fields. He also purposely instructed his reapers to leave extra for her to glean.

The Path of Life

After Ruth's mother-in-law gave her some instruction about the customs of the Israelites, Ruth obediently carried out all that she had been told to do. Boaz was grateful for the kindness she had repaid him, so he opened the way for them to become husband and wife.

Boaz planned to meet the relative who was a closer relative than he was. He said to him:

> *"Naomi, who has come back from the country of Moab,*
> *sold the piece of land which belonged*
> *to our brother Elimelech.*
> *On the day you buy the field from the hand of Naomi,*
> *you must also buy it from Ruth the Moabitess."*
>
> Ruth 4:3, 5a

When the older brother of Boaz chose not to take the inheritance, this allowed Boaz to redeem the right to claim the land, look after Naomi, and marry Ruth.

Ruth had lived in Moab where Baal was worshipped, and had married Marlon, the son of Naomi, but he had died. Ruth returned with Naomi to start a new life, unaware that she too was part of the plan the Lord had prepared. Ruth had also embraced the God of Naomi and worshipped Him. Boaz, like his father, had no misconceptions about Ruth and took her as his wife. Ruth was like both her mothers-in-law, who were grateful for all that was afforded to her.

Further Insights: Jericho and Beyond

Boaz and Ruth had a son whom they named Obed, who grew up and also had a son whom they called Jesse. Jesse had eight sons, the youngest one was called David, who would become the anointed king of Israel.

King David had several sons with his wives and concubines and four sons with his wife Bathsheba, Shammua, Shobab, Nathan and Solomon (1 Chronicles 3:5). Solomon and Nathan both had many descendants and after eight hundred years had passed, a distant relative of Solomon by the name of Joseph, met a distant relative of Nathan called Mary in the city of Nazareth.

The Angel Gabriel visited Mary when she was betrothed to Joseph and told her about the plan of the Lord for her and her husband-to-be. While Mary did not completely understand what was expected, she willingly obeyed as did Joseph.

In the town of Bethlehem, as was prophesied, Mary gave birth to a Son whom they called Jesus, who became the Saviour of the world, providing salvation for mankind. As Jesus grew and fulfilled His divine calling, He suffered and died for the sins of mankind. As He was raised from the dead, and the way for the Holy Spirit made open, the third promise all those years earlier to Abram was fulfilled.

The answer was certainly not what the Jews (Israelites) expected, but then is anything with the Lord answered with our expectation? The three promises given were fulfilled as God is a promise keeper, not a liar. We should be grateful for what Jesus accomplished for us and never complain about our circumstances, but in all things, give thanks with a grateful heart.

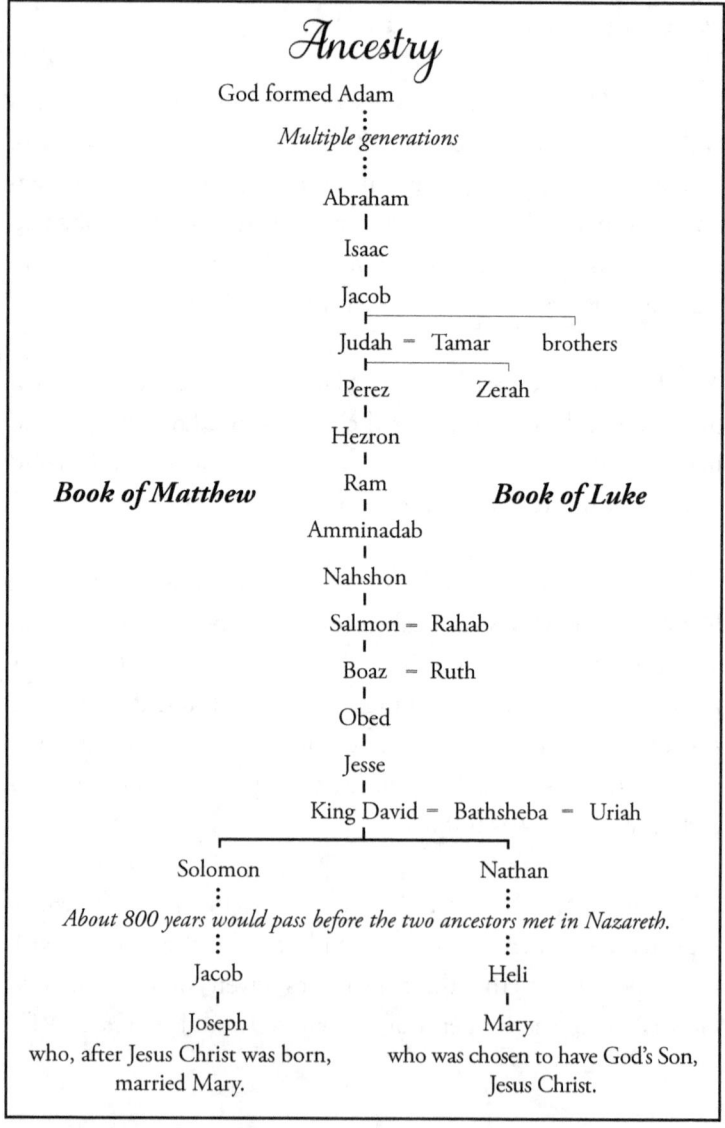

The Southern Conquest

With the defeat and the destruction of Jericho, Joshua and the children of Israel were ready to move forward. They knew the Lord was with them and His protection was theirs. As Jericho was no more, the children of Israel advanced to take and secure Ai which would not be a concern to them, but as no one was unaware of the sin of Achan, Israel suffered a major defeat, not only in battle but in their faith and trust in the Lord. When the sin was dealt with, Israel approached Ai but in a different light.

When Ai was finally conquered through ambush after the first attempt failed, Joshua was ready to move through the southern kingdom one city at a time, as the Israelites were once more assured of the presence of the Lord and His protection.

City by city was conquered, as no one could defeat the children of Israel. Makkedah was followed by, Libnah, Lachish, Gezer, Eglon, Hebron, and Debir. Joshua and the Israelites conquered the mountain country, the lowlands and the wilderness slopes, from Kadesh Barnea as far as Gaza and all the country of Goshen, even as far as Gibeon.

It must have been an eerie feeling for the Israelites to arrive at Goshen, the city vacated by their parents over forty-five years previously. When Moses led the children of Israel out for the three-day hike into the desert where sacrifice to the God of the Hebrews would be carried out, the whole city of Goshen would have become a ghost town and remained that way for some time.

Other people from various regions, could have secured a home for themselves and eventually, the city of Goshen became a community of various religions and people who worshipped many deities.

The land of Goshen would have contained many bad memories for the Egyptians, as they were told by parents and grandparents of the pain and suffering inflicted on them through the Pharaoh who refused to bow to the God of the Hebrews, but in the end, conceded defeat.

How many widows and fatherless children, who were now grown adults, chose not to go to the land of Goshen under any circumstance? The once mighty nation of Egypt never rose again to the heights they had previously enjoyed and experienced. How the dictatorship of one person had shattered lives by wrong decisions, choices the people had no control over, but wore the consequence.

As the fighting men of the Israelites attacked Goshen and its gods, where were the Egyptians? Although Goshen was a nearby suburb of Egypt, the Egyptians were nowhere to be found. No aid was evident to those of Goshen in their time of need or suffering.

Further Insights: The Southern Conquest

Some years previous, when Phineas the son of Eliezer attacked Midian, killed their five kings, their fighting men, and plundered their livestock and cities, the Egyptians did not come to their aid either. God had dealt severely with Pharaoh because as Jethro had said,

> *"Blessed be the Lord,*
> *who has delivered you out of the hand of Pharaoh,*
> *and who has delivered the people*
> *from under the hand of the Egyptians.*
> *Now I know that the Lord is greater than all the gods;*
> *for in the very thing in which they behaved proudly,*
> *He was above them."*
>
> Exodus 18:10–11

Pride always came before a fall; Pharaoh and the Egyptians were no exception. The writer of Proverbs and Isaiah said similar words used by James, the earthly brother of Jesus, and Peter, in his first epistle when they wrote:

> *"God resists the proud,*
> *but gives grace to the humble."*
>
> James 4:6b

Foreshadows of Jesus

The complete writings about God's chosen people are all about Jesus His Son, from the encounter of the Lord with Abram, then Melchizedek, to the fulfilment of the three promises given to Abram. The question to be asked is, "Who was Melchizedek?" The writer to the Hebrews sheds light on this priest from Salem, which was the former name of Jerusalem. As the priest of the Most High God, meaning *'King of Righteousness'*, and king of Salem, meaning *'King of Peace'*, we are further told:

> *"Without father, without mother,*
> *without genealogy, having neither*
> *beginning of days not end of life,*
> *but made like the Son of God,*
> *remains a priest continually."*

Hebrews 7:3

Many years later, Paul wrote to the Philippians and said, *"Who being in the form of God, did not consider it robbery to be equal with God, but made Himself of no reputation, taking the form of a bond-servant, and coming in the likeness of men. And*

being found in appearance as a man, He humbled Himself and became obedient to the point of death, even the death of the cross."
Philippians 2:6–8

John the disciple of Jesus, the earthly cousin of Jesus, proclaimed the following.

"In the beginning was the Word,
and the Word was with God,
and the Word was God.
He was in the beginning with God.
All things were made through Him,
and without Him nothing was made that was made."

John 1:1–3

Jesus is the *'Word'*, the Working part of God. While the Holy Spirit is the Power of God given to men, Jesus has been active from the creation of the world, when He spoke everything into being, until we share eternity with Him in the New Heavens and the New Earth in the New Jerusalem. The Bible provides clear evidence that Melchizedek was Jesus in an earthly form, who walked and talked with Abram.

Moses encountered another form of Jesus at the burning bush, where the plans for Moses were laid out to him and the fulfilment of the promises previously given to his ancestor Abram. Jesus accompanied Moses in his journey as He communicated to

Him, what He would bring to pass. The most significant of the plagues was the last, as this was all about Jesus and His fulfilment for the eternal destiny of mankind.

Before the last plague was instituted, the 'Passover Meal' was to be prepared and eaten in a specific way. Let us note the similarities between the preparation and the completion of the meal.

> Overleaf: Chart - The Passover & Jesus' Fulfilment

To demonstrate the power that Jesus had at His disposal to Moses, the following is written.

> *"It is the Lord's Passover.*
> *For I will pass through the land of Egypt on that night,*
> *and will strike all the firstborn in the land of Egypt,*
> *both man and beast;*
> *and against all the gods of Egypt*
> *I will execute judgement:*
> *I am the Lord."*
>
> Exodus 12:11b–12

John records the words of Jesus when He said,

The Path of Life

The Passover	*Jesus' Fulfilment*
A Lamb chosen four days before. Exodus 12:3	Jesus rode into Jerusalem four days before Passover. John 12:9–16
A Lamb without Blemish. Exodus 12:5	Jesus was without blemish. He was without sin. 1 Peter 1:18–19
A lamb one year old. Exodus 12:3	Jesus was a in the prime of His life. Isaiah 53:7
A lamb was to be male. Exodus 12:5	Jesus came to earth as a male. Philippians 2:8
Each family was to share in the meal. Exodus 12:3–4	Each person is required to take of Jesus to receive life. Acts 4:12
The Passover lamb was to be killed at twilight. Exodus 12:6	Jesus died at 3 pm. Mark 15:25, 31–38
Nothing was to be left. Exodus 12:10	Jesus was taken down from the cross and laid in the tomb. John 19:31
The lamb was killed for the life of the firstborn Israelite. Exodus 12:12	Jesus died in our place. Romans 8:29
The shed blood was a sign of redemption. Exodus 12:7, 12–13	Jesus' blood covers our sin. We are right before God. Romans 5:8–10
The blood on the door posts. Exodus 12:21–23	Jesus sacrifice sets us free from the bondage of sin. Romans 8:1–2.
The lamb was to be eaten entirely. Exodus 12:10	We need to abide in Jesus and learn from Him continually. John 15:4–5
The Passover opened the way to freedom. Exodus 12:31–32	The only way to Jesus is through His shed blood. John 5:24

> *"I have the power to lay my life down,*
> *and I have the power to take it up again.*
> *This command I have received from My Father."*
>
> John 10:18b

As Jesus has the power of life and death, He moved across the land of Egypt and fulfilled the known will of God. To the Egyptians it meant death, but to those who obeyed the instructions given to them by Moses, it meant life.

Moses continued to be guided by the pillar of cloud by day and the pillar of fire by night to show the way they were to travel. At the Red Sea, the cloud moved between the Israelites and the Egyptians, as the cloud provided light to the Israelites, but the Egyptians were in darkness. A verse Jesus shared could apply to the Egyptians:

> *"For everyone practising evil*
> *hates the light and does not come to the light,*
> *lest his deeds should be exposed."*
>
> John 3:20

When the pillar of cloud gave light to the Israelites, the words Jesus related to them could have been:

> *"I am the light of the world.*
> *He who follows Me*

shall not walk in darkness,
but have the light of life."

John 8:12

Both these preceding verses could be applied during the ninth plague, that of darkness, but just as the cloud separated and protected the children of Israel from the Egyptians, the way was made open for the Israelites to cross over to freedom by faith through the waters to life. David, the shepherd boy wrote some verses about Jesus and His protection:

"Yea, though I walk through the valley
of the shadow of death,
I will fear no evil;
for You are with me;
Your rod and staff,
they comfort me."

Psalm 23:4

Just as Moses stretched out his rod over the water to part the sea, the way to freedom from oppression, slavery, and bondage was opened. The Israelites had a choice to stay or go. They were told but not compelled to travel the way the Lord had provided, but the rod corrected those who would not follow, and the staff provided the protection all required to experience. As Jesus is the Way, the Truth and the Life (John 14:6), on another occasion He said:

"I have come that they may have life,
and that they may have it more abundantly."

John 10:10b

Those who crossed over passed from death to life. While the focus was on the Promised Land and all it held for them, there was always an in-between to encounter. When the children of Israel had travelled three days into the Wilderness of Shur, they found no water but the bitter waters of Marah. As the Israelites complained to Moses, the Lord showed him a tree which they cut down and threw into the waters which became sweet.

The Lord told them that if they listened to His voice and followed His commandments, He would provide for them, not only in health but in everything they required. The branch represented the transforming power of Jesus, once we have been grafted into Him, the *Vine*. Jesus would further substantiate this when He said:

"I am the vine, you are the branches.
He who abides in Me, and I in him,
bears much fruit;
for without Me you can do nothing."

John 15:5

When Jesus was talking with the woman at the well, He shared with her about living waters. Jesus continued to teach that:

> *"God is a Spirit,*
> *and those who worship Him*
> *must worship in spirit and truth."*
>
> John 4:24

The transformed life, which is joined with Jesus, is not self-focused but God-focused, through the power of Jesus. This was just the first lesson of many the children of Israel would be subject to. While they were guided and had everything supplied, the truth appeared to evade the majority.

The children of Israel continued to Elim and camped around twelve wells of water and seventy palm trees. This time was one of rest, where they had all their needs supplied as they pondered their entry into the promised land and reflected on the past. Words of Jesus suit this occasion when He said:

> *"Come unto Me,*
> *all you who labour and are heavy laden,*
> *and I will give you rest.*
> *Take My yoke upon you and learn from Me,*
> *for I am gentle and lowly in heart,*
> *and you will find rest for your souls.*
> *For My yoke is easy and My burden is light."*
>
> Matthew 11:28–30

Their next move was into the Wilderness of Sin, which was between Elim and Sinai, and they were now in their second month since they left Egypt. Hunger was a major issue so they complained to Moses and Aaron, but really, they were complaining about the Lord not providing for their needs. Exodus 16:2

Our prayers and petitions are always heard by Father God, but the answer we receive is very rarely what we had in mind as the solution to our petition. Quail was provided for the whole camp and in the morning came the Manna. They had never experienced what was provided, for as they looked after the mist had risen, there on the ground was this semi-transparent colour seed like that of the coriander. Numbers 11:7

When they inquired about collecting and usage, specific instructions followed. Even though some gathered more than they required which inhibited others from obtaining enough, when they were measured out, everyone had the same (Exodus 16:18). This was all about obedience to the revealed or known will of God, which was a lesson this generation of the children of Israel never learnt.

The Lord moved the camp to Rephidim, but there was no water for the people to drink, so they complained to Moses, about provision. They had stopped trusting the Lord and were looking to Moses the man as their source and provider as they were ready to stone him. Moses took some of the elders and the people and stood before the rock in Horeb. Because the Lord stood before Moses on the rock, when he struck the rock, water came out for the people and their livestock to drink.

As manna and water were both provided, we can couple them with the words of Jesus when He taught the crowds in Capernaum about Himself when He said:

> *"I am the bread of life.*
> *He who comes to Me shall never hunger,*
> *and he who believes in Me*
> *shall never thirst."*
>
> John 6:35

The chosen people never understood who provided for them in their need. This misunderstanding travelled through time because Jesus also tried to correct the wrong thinking of His day that it was not Moses, but the Father who provided all things to those who believed.

Three months had passed since the Israelites had left Egypt, and they were not in the promised land, but camped in the Wilderness of Sinai, before Mount Sinai. The time had arrived to covenant with the children of Israel who had been called to be His special people, dedicated to the Lord (Deuteronomy 7:6). Up until now, everyone had acted with what they saw was right in their eyes and understanding. This was about to be refined as to what God required of His chosen people. The words previously used, spoken by Jesus could refer to the law that was about to be given to them as the invitation was to:

> *"Take My yoke upon you and learn from Me,*
> *for I am gentle and lowly in heart,*
> *and you will find rest for your souls."*
>
> Matthew 11:29

After they agreed with the presented covenant, Moses and Joshua ascended the mountain to receive the Law from God. When they returned after forty days, the children of Israel had broken the first three laws they had agreed to. Although the Lord wanted to consume the people, Moses pleaded for them and the Lord relented but would hold them accountable in the future.

As the Law was now in place, to be found righteous in the sight of God, all must keep the given law continuously. As this was an impossibility for earthly-born man, God provided His Son Jesus, not born of the will of man, but of God. Jesus was born of the Holy Spirit with the tendency not to sin as man was born in sin inherited through Adam. Jesus referred to the Law when He said:

> *"I did not come to destroy*
> *the Law or the Prophets.*
> *I did not come to destroy but to fulfil."*
>
> Matthew 5:17

Jesus said to His disciples:

> *"I am the way, the truth, and the life.*
> *No one comes to the Father*
> *except through Me."*
>
> John 14:6

The time had arrived to build a suitable dwelling place for the presence of the Lord to manifest Himself, so the Tabernacle was built and constructed with the expressed instruction given to Moses. When the Tabernacle was completed and inspected by Moses as a fit dwelling place for the Lord to inhabit:

> *"Then the cloud covered the*
> *Tabernacle of Meeting,*
> *and the Glory of the Lord*
> *filled the Tabernacle."*
>
> Exodus 40:34

As all the past events of the journey of the Israelites represented Jesus, so too does the Tabernacle. Everything about the Tabernacle reflected Jesus, as it was all about Him. We see the reflection in the seven main items placed in the Tabernacle area and inside the Tabernacle, as each reflected what Jesus had said when referring to Himself. The list of seven items is as follows:

- The Brazen Altar.   John 10:11
- The Laver.   John 11:25–26
- The Doorway.   John 10:9
- The Golden Candlesticks.   John 8:12
- The Shewbread Table.   John 6:35
- The Incense Altar.   John 15:5
- The Holy of Holies.   John 14:6

The children of Israel had embraced all the teachings about the Tabernacle as they journeyed from Egypt to Mount Sinai, as everything they had experienced pointed to the Lamb of God. Everything was about obedience and what was expected of covenanted people, not of people who were self-focused.

The Lord still had a couple of opportunities to relate His Son to them but in a different way, and something they had never anticipated. The Census produced a document of the number of people and their tribes. Twelve tribes and the Levites. Thirteen areas in total. When the tribes were arranged in the designated areas, they formed a cross. This was prophetic, as no one would have understood what the future would reflect for them and the Saviour who this whole journey is about.

Moses was instructed to set up the seven feasts they were to observe. The seven feasts are:

- The Passover Feast.
- The Feast of Unleavened Bread.
- The Feast of Firstfruits.
- The Feast of Weeks.
- The Feast of Trumpets.
- Yon Kippur or Day of Atonement.
- The Feast of Tabernacles.

Just as the Tabernacle reflected Jesus and what He said, so too did the Feasts. Each Feast represented teaching and paralleled with each other. So, what did they represent?

- The Brazen Altar represented the 'Passover', as the lamb was slain, and offered as a sacrifice, and the blood, along with the ashes were used in the remission of sins.
- The Laver represented the 'Feast of Unleavened Bread' as no leaven was used when the bread was made. Leaven always referred to sin, so the removal of leaven symbolised the removal of sin, because of the sacrifice made.
- The Doorway, represented the 'Feast of Firstfruits', because the lamb had been slain, and sin removed, the priest could go into the Holy Place and carry out the necessary duties, as he had been washed clean.
- The Golden Candlesticks represented the 'Feast of Weeks', that would be set up in the future, as the name changed to 'Pentecost', as those of the called received the power to live their life.

- The Shewbread Table represented another future feast that would be set up, the 'Feast of Trumpets'.

- The Incense Altar represented the 'Day of Atonement' or Yon Kippur, when the priest would take the blood and the ashes of the sacrificed animal by the priest, into the Holy of Holies, on one designated day and the people would receive forgiveness for the sin they had committed.

- The Holy of Holies housed the presence of God, and was associated with the 'Feast of Tabernacles'. This feast also portrayed the hardship conditions the children of Israel, endured during the forty years in the wilderness.

The Tabernacle centred on the 'Feasts of Israel', but also about Jesus Christ, the foretold Messiah. As the Lord ordained and fashioned the Tabernacle, it was designed to reflect Jesus in every way. All the items were to be made in the strictest sense, without blemish.

The Tabernacle	*The Feasts of Israel*	*The I AMs*
The Brazen Altar	The Passover Feast	I am the good shepherd
The Laver	The Feast of Unleavened Bread	I am the resurrection and the life
The Doorway	The Feast of Firstfruits	I am the door
The Golden Candlesticks	The Feast of Weeks	I am the light of the world
The Shewbread Table	The Feast of Trumpets	I am the bread of life
The Incense Altar	Yon Kippur (Day of Atonement)	I am the vine
Holy of Holies	The Feast of Tabernacles	I am the way, the truth and the life

Only Passover was celebrated until after the children of Israel entered the promised land as we read:

"Speak to the children of Israel,

and say to them:

'When you come into the land which I give to you,

and reap its harvest, then you shall bring

a sheaf of the Firstfruits of your harvest to the priest.'"

Leviticus 23:10

In the first month of the second year since the children of Israel had left Egypt, as they were still camped at Mount Sinai, Moses instructed the children of Israel to observe the Passover. This they carried out in remembrance with gratitude of what they had been delivered from.

The Tabernacle and the teaching of Moses were a continual reminder of the presence of the Lord. But after about thirty-three years spent wandering in the desert, they still grumbled, but this was no ordinary grumble as they spoke against Moses and the Lord.

"Why have you brought us up out of Egypt
to die in the wilderness?
For there is no food and no water,
and our soul loathes this worthless bread."

Numbers 21:5

As this happened in the latter part of their forty years of wandering in the desert, a younger generation was making their presence felt as most of the older generation were now dead. This brought a quick response as fiery serpents invaded the camp. While many died, some cried out to Moses, repenting for their sins against Moses and the Lord. Their repentant prayer was heard and a solution was applied. The Lord told Moses to:

"Make a fiery bronze serpent,
and set it on a pole;

> *and it shall be that everyone who is bitten,*
> *when he looks at it, shall live."*
>
> Numbers 21:8

The message was to look and live. Jesus would later proclaim to the crowds:

> *"As Moses lifted up the serpent in the wilderness,*
> *even so must the Son of Man be lifted up,*
> *that whoever believes in Him*
> *should not perish but have eternal life."*
>
> John 3:14–15

Just as the Israelites were required to look and live, so too were those who Jesus came to save as He said:

> *"For the Son of Man has come*
> *to seek and to save the lost."*
>
> Luke 19:10

One of the last things that reflects Jesus is correctly diving the word, or making sure while we have wisdom, we understand what is asked. Moses was nearing the end of his journey, and he faulted. The children of Israel again complained about no water and blamed Moses. It had been about thirty-five years since the slaves left Egypt, and no land flowing with milk and honey had been claimed. This was not what they had expected, although they did not consider their constant grumbling and disobedience when told to go in and take the promised land.

Moses was told to speak to the rock and that water would come out, but he spoke harshly to the people and struck the rock twice. Moses had failed to open the new avenue through which the Lord intended to move. As he acted based on experience that had worked then, the Lord was displeased with his actions. The measure of success in the Lord's eyes is not the outcome of the effort, but the obedience of His servant.

This sin of disobedience did not exclude Moses from entering into his heavenly eternal rest. His sin was covered by the sacrificial system in place. After Moses viewed the promised land, he died and the Lord buried him in a valley in the land of Moab opposite Beth Peor. But the story of Moses does not end with his death, for we read the following:

> "Michael the archangel,
> in contending with the devil,
> when he disputed about the body of Moses,
> dared not bring against him a reviling accusation,
> but said, 'The Lord rebuke you!'"
>
> Jude 9

Michael won this battle as we read later the following:

The Path of Life

> *"As Jesus was transfigured before*
> *Peter, James, and John,*
> *His face shone like the sun,*
> *and His clothes became as white as light.*
> *And behold,*
> *Moses and Elijah appeared to them,*
> *talking with Him."*
>
> Matthew 17:2–3

Moses had reflected on the future life of Jesus as many similarities are found in the accounts told about both their lives. Moses established the Law, whereas Jesus came to fulfil the Law, not destroy the law. While the Israelites were dying of thirst in the desert, Moses struck a rock, and from the blow, it yielded water to quench their thirst. Similarly, while we are dying of spiritual thirst in the desert of spiritual alienation from God, God struck a better Rock, the Rock *Christ Jesus* for our sins, so we can obtain *Living Water* to quench our thirst of spiritual alienation from God.

Similarities Between Moses and Jesus

MOSES	JESUS
Pharaoh ordered mass killing of new born male boys.	King Herod ordered mass killing of babies under 2 years of age.
Moses was placed in a basket for safety.	Jesus was laid in a manger for safety.
Moses was taught the essence of Egyptian culture.	Jesus was taught the Torah, Psalms and Prophets in the synagogues.
Moses was a descendant of Jacob, a Levite.	Jesus was a descendant of Jacob, a Judean.
Moses led the Israelites out of Egyptian bondage.	Jesus led the called out of bondage to sin.
Moses received the Ten Commandments.	Jesus reinterpreted the commandments in the Sermon on the Mount.
Moses carried the Law and pointed to the Gospel.	Jesus fulfilled the Law and is the Gospel.
Moses broke the 400 years of bondage to the Egyptians.	Jesus broke the 400 years of silence from Father God.
Moses offered excuses for not completing God's will.	Jesus was victorious over Satan to complete God's will.
Moses left his royal position to be with his own.	Jesus left His Father and became a man to redeem the called.
Moses was seen as an Egyptian but had the heart of a Hebrew.	Jesus was both God and man as He was One with the Father.
Moses heard God speak through an unconsumed burning bush.	Jesus speaks to us through His Death and Resurrection.
Moses was used to part the Red Sea.	Jesus calmed the wind and waves on the Sea of Galilee.
Moses chose 12 spies and sent them into the Promised Land.	Jesus chose 12 disciples to take the message of salvation to the world.
Moses prayed to God for Manna and Quail for the Israelites.	Jesus fed the 5,000 Jews and the 4,000 Gentiles.

MOSES	JESUS
Moses received God's Covenant.	Jesus instituted the New Covenant.
Moses was the author of the Law and the first mediator.	Jesus fulfilled the Law and is our Great High Priest.
Moses built the Tabernacle to show the presence of God.	Jesus provided the Holy Spirit to fill us with His presence.
Moses lifted up the pole and snake for people to look and live.	Jesus was lifted up to draw the called unto Himself, to remove death's sting.
Moses initiated the Passover Lamb to save the first born.	Jesus is the Passover Lamb, the Christ to save all who come to Him.
Moses turned water into blood.	Jesus turned water into wine.
Moses struck the rock to give the Israelites water.	Jesus provides living water through the Holy Spirit to the spiritual thirsty.
Moses led the Israelites to the Promised Land.	Jesus leads the called to the New Jerusalem and eternal life.

Jesus was further revealed through Joshua, but to a lesser extent. The Book of Joshua points us to Jesus, the real hero of God's Word and our life. Joshua's story is about God's promised faithfulness in the past, present and future. The God we serve has been working on the story of His Son Jesus, for thousands of years. Like Joshua and Caleb, we need to be the ones with faith, faith through whatever comes our way knowing it is the plan of God for each of us.

Joshua, who led the children of Israel, the Lord's chosen into the Promised Land, reflected Jesus, who leads the faithful into the ultimate land of promise, the Celestial Kingdom. As there are no surprises to God, let us each claim the confession of Joshua when he said:

Foreshadows of Jesus

"But as for me and my household, we will serve the Lord."

Joshua 24:15b.

Joshua, a Foreshadowing of Jesus

JOSHUA	JESUS
The name Joshua.	Jesus' name in Hebrew is 'Yeshua' which translated to English is Joshua.
Joshua means *saves*.	'Yeshua' means *God saves*.
Joshua fulfilled the foretold prophesies.	Jesus fulfilled the foretold will of the Father.
Joshua led to the promised land to Israel.	Jesus leads to the Promised Land of heaven.
Joshua led the Children into the Promised Land.	Jesus led captivity captive.
Joshua defeated the enemies of the Israelites.	Jesus defeated the enemy, sin and death
Joshua saw victory when the trumpets blew and the shout came at Jericho.	Jesus will bring final victory when the trumpets blow and the shouts come when He returns.
Joshua pointed to the way of God as obedience to the will of God.	Jesus said He is the way, the truth and the life.
Joshua helped to fulfil the promises to those of God's calling.	Jesus calls to those who are of the called to receive eternal life.
Joshua wrote the Law of God on stone for all to remember and be aware.	Jesus fulfilled the Law and offered Grace to the whosoever.

Joshua established the feast of Israel, which is all about gratitude and thankfulness to Father God for all He does in our life. The reflection of Jesus would always be known through the feasts as they were celebrated annually. Throughout history, the Jews have completed the feasts but with some modifications when Jerusalem was demolished, and blood sacrifice was discontinued, the Jews found other ways to commemorate the Feasts.

Jesus instituted or replaced the old *Covenant of the Law*, with a *New Covenant of Grace*. In the Old Covenant, all things were remembered and celebrated out of gratitude for what the Lord had completed for their redemption. Jesus said to His disciples, and to all those who truly believe and accepted Jesus as their Lord and Saviour,

> *"Take, eat; this is My body*
> *which is broken for you;*
> *do this in remembrance of Me."*
> *In the same manner*
> *He also took the cup after supper, saying,*
> *"This cup is the new covenant in My blood.*
> *This do, as often as you drink it,*
> *in remembrance of Me."*
>
> 1 Corinthians 11:24–25

The Path of Life

The children of Israel are now settled in their new home. Have the promises made to Abram, so many years earlier,

> "I will give you a land of your own;
> I will make you a great nation;
> I will bless you and in you
> all the families of the earth will be blessed,"
>
> Genesis 12:1–3

been established through Abram's encounter with Melchizedek, Moses leading the Hebrews through the wilderness and Joshua leading them into Canaan?

To bring some clarification to the promises, the following verse reveals a truth that has been so far overlooked.

> "And I will establish My covenant
> between Me and you (Abram)
> and your descendants after you
> in their generations,

> *for an everlasting covenant,*
> *to be God to you and your*
> *descendants after you."*
>
> Genesis 17:7

In verse thirteen of the same chapter God says, *"My covenant shall be in your flesh for an everlasting covenant,"* and in verse nineteen God says:

> *"I will establish My covenant with him*
> *for an everlasting covenant,*
> *and with his descendants after him."*
>
> Genesis 17:19

The three promises or covenant which the Lord outlined to Abram, was not something that would be accomplished in a short time. Each of the three promises would continue until the return of Jesus:

> *"While the earth remains,*
> *seedtime and harvest, cold and heat,*
> *winter and summer, and day and night*
> *shall not cease."*
>
> Genesis 8:22

The Covenant with Abram was a perpetual or everlasting covenant which meant it had no end while the earth remained, as the three promises would continue to be fulfilled. While the promises are partially completed, the fulfilment is in the future.

This was not the first time these three promises were given by the Lord. When the Lord formed Adam, He gave him a land of his own, in the garden of Eden to care for and tend, a wife by the name of Eve, and together they would become a mighty nation of priests who would be a blessing to the world. They were also given the law and told not to eat from the tree of the knowledge of good and evil: one law, not ten.

As Adam and Eve had broken the one law that the Lord had ordained, the sacrificial system was introduced to cover their sin. Animal sacrifice was instituted, as the shedding of blood not only covered their sin, but the skins provided were a covering for them both. The Lord had set in place the destiny of sinful man who had the tendency to sin, but through true repentance, would find his sin forgiven and restoration would take place.

When Adam and Eve yielded to the temptation, their sin broke the covenant, so judgment was passed on them and all who would follow. Their descendants would become a mighty nation with a land of their own, but not in the foreseeable future. The Lord would choose a few as a 'priesthood of believers', to bless the world through the Son of God, Jesus, born through the bloodline of Adam.

As time progressed, the Lord saw that the heart of man was evil.

> "Then the Lord saw that the wickedness
> of man was great in the earth,
> and that every intent of the thoughts
> of his heart was only evil continually."
>
> Genesis 6:5

The Lord passed judgment on the then-known world and destroyed all the inhabitants except for Noah and his household. After the flood subsided, the Lord made two covenants, the first was with creation:

> "While the earth remains,
> seedtime and harvest, cold and heat,
> winter and summer,
> and day and night shall not cease."
>
> Genesis 8:22

The second covenant was with Noah, his sons and all their descendants as well as every living creature that was with them. The Lord said:

> "Never again shall all flesh be cut off
> by the waters of the flood;
> never again shall there be a flood
> to destroy the earth.

> *This is the sign of the covenant*
> *which I make between Me and you.*
> *I set my rainbow in the cloud,*
> *and it shall be a sign of the covenant*
> *between Me and you."*
>
> Genesis 9:11, v13

When the children of Noah began to multiply, they chose to make a name for themselves. Seeking fame and glory and ignoring the Lord as their provider, they failed to worship Him. The Lord was swift to pass judgment on the people, confused their language then scattered them everywhere throughout the then-known world, which was the very thing they feared.

The Lord chose Abram to fulfil His plan and purpose as he was in the bloodline of Adam, even though a little less than two thousand years had passed. Abram was called upon to rescue his nephew Lot from the enemy who had taken him captive and many others from the city of Sodom. Abram had the victory as he brought back all the goods, the people and his nephew. As Lot chose to return to the city of Sodom, Melchizedek the priest of God Most High, brought bread and wine and met with Abram and blessed him.

> *"Blessed be Abram of God Most High,*
> *Possessor of heaven and earth;*
> *and blessed be God Most High,*

> *Who has delivered your enemies*
>
> *into your hand."*
>
> Genesis 14:19–20

The king of Sodom also met with Abram and said, *"Give me the persons, and take the goods for yourself"* (Genesis 14:21). But Abram said to the king of Sodom:

> *"I have raised my hand to the Lord,*
>
> *God Most High,*
>
> *the Possessor of heaven and earth,*
>
> *that I will take nothing,*
>
> *from a thread to a sandal strap,*
>
> *and that I will not take anything that is yours,*
>
> *lest you should say,*
>
> *'I have made Abram rich'."*
>
> Genesis 14:22-23

The cities of Sodom and Gomorrah were wicked cities, harbouring people with many ungodly sexual desires. The fact that Lot chose to return to this city, says much about him and his beliefs, but there is more to be found in this event. Abram had made allegiance to the God Most High through Melchizedek, and then the king of Sodom suggested a counteroffer.

The Path of Life

Abram, after he rescued Lot is similar to Jesus saving a person from the grip of sin. Just as Lot chose to go back and live in the city of Sodom, some who have been rescued from the depths of sin go back to their old way of life, choosing death over life.

About two thousand years in the future, Jesus was offered three options from Satan (Matthew 4:1–11). Abram is represented by Jesus and the king of Sodom as Satan. Abram would accept nothing from the king, just as Jesus in the future, knew His allegiance was to the Father. Just as the city of Sodom was destroyed by the Lord, so too shall the domain of Satan be obliterated and thrown into the Lake of Fire with all those who have followed him.

The Lord gave Abram three promises, but the fulfilment would be a long way in the future. The promises are also spiritual, which means each has a parallel in the spiritual realm. While the children of Israel conquered Canaan, after they had eradicated most of their distant cursed relatives, they did not teach those in the portions of land allotted to them about their God or instituted laws and practises He required. Instead, they compromised and joined in with the gods the people worshipped.

In the future, those of the called will live in the New Heavens, and the New Earth in the New Jerusalem, and will fellowship with the Father, the Son and the Holy Spirit, as old things will pass away and all things will become new.

Judges were appointed, and kings anointed by prophets to lead the children of Israel. The spiritual fervour of the people depended on the king and his allegiance to the Lord. If the king was corrupt and worshipped false gods, then the people suffered, but the kings who were aware of the power of the Lord, through the indwelling presence of the Holy Spirit, were protected and prospered.

The kings, over many years, continued to guide the chosen people in their evil ways, but the prophets encouraged the people to turn back to God and seek forgiveness. While King Saul ruled well, he also faulted as the Lord said:

> *"I greatly regret that I have set up Saul as king,*
> *for he has turned back from following Me,*
> *and has not performed My commandments."*
>
> 1 Samuel 15:11

The Lord directed Samuel the prophet, to anoint David the next king of Israel, as it was written of him:

> *"David did what was right in the eyes of the Lord,*
> *and had not turned aside from anything*
> *that He commanded him all the days of his life,*
> *except in the matter of Uriah the Hittite."*
>
> 1 Kings 15:5

In 2 Samuel 7:8–16, 1 Chronicles 17:1–27, reference is made to the covenant. In Psalms, David also referred to the everlasting covenant, the Abrahamic covenant.

> *"He remembers His covenant forever,*
> *the word which He commanded,*
> *for a thousand generations,*
> *the covenant which He made with Abraham,*
> *and His oath to Isaac,*
> *and confirmed it to Jacob for a statute,*
> *to Israel as an everlasting covenant."*
>
> Psalms 105:8–10

The next time the everlasting covenant is mentioned is by the prophets, Isaiah 24:1–5, Jeremiah 32:40, and Ezekiel 16:60–63, as God spoke through them prophetically about their future. The Lord said:

> *"You shall no longer be termed forsaken,*
> *nor shall your land any more be termed desolate,*
> *for the Lord delights in you.*
> *So shall your God rejoice over you."*
>
> Isaiah 62: 4–5

The entire chapter of Jeremiah 31 is God speaking about the covenant He had with His people. The story is told of Israel's departure from serving God, and their punishment for that sin. The children of Israel had often reverted to their old ways, as in the days of rule under Pharaoh, worshipped many pagan gods. A remnant always remained faithful to the Lord, although they were in the minority. Has anything changed with our church leadership? Are they walking by faith or sight? The Lord is always present with and to the faithful remnant, to guide, teach and protect.

Those who are religious leaders in Jerusalem today, pursue a different plan than that of Father God, by building a new temple and once again re-establishing the old religious system, but they have been deceived as Jeremiah foretold the coming of Jesus and the establishment of a new covenant.

"Behold, the days are coming, says the Lord, when I will make a new covenant with the house of Israel and with the house of Judah, not according to the covenant that I made with their fathers in the day that I took them by the hand to lead them out of the land of Egypt, My covenant which they broke, though I was a husband to them, says the Lord. But this is the covenant that I will make with the house of Israel after those days, says the Lord: I will put My law in their minds, and write it on their hearts; and I will be their God, and they shall be My people.

"No more shall every man teach his neighbour, and every man his brother, saying, 'Know the Lord,' for they all shall know Me, from the least of them to the greatest of them, says the Lord. For I

will forgive their iniquity, and their sin I will remember no more." Jeremiah 31:31–34

The children of Israel grew in numbers as the years passed, but a mighty nation that would rule the world never came to fruition. Because they had turned away from wholly serving the Lord, they were defeated by others and taken captive into foreign countries where they were subject to the gods of their land. All through history, they have been a persecuted race, always looking for the time when they would be recognised as God's chosen.

While a remnant survived, taught, and observed the feasts and what Father God ordained, modification to their religion eroded the essence of a holy people, till today, they have a form of religion but are certainly denying the power. In the future, those who have been chosen by God shall be His kingdom of priests, reigning with Him forever in the heavenly places.

Israel continues to manufacture and develop much in the material world, which has certainly brought many blessings, but two thousand years ago, they denied the spiritual blessing offered to them by the Son of God, Jesus Christ. Because they rejected Jesus, they opened the way for the Gentiles to be grafted into the body of Christ, and through the preaching of the Gospel, many have been and are blessed.

Many prophets were sent to guide the children of Israel back to the God of Abraham, Isaac, and Jacob. However, they saw those who brought the messages as 'Prophets of Doom', and while some accepted the teaching, the majority had hardened their hearts to the warning to repent and turn back to God. The Lord continued sending prophets but they killed many as Jesus would say:

> *"From the blood of Abel to the blood of Zechariah*
> *who perished between the altar and the temple."*
>
> Luke 11:51a

Because the Lord knew the heart of man as he continued to sin and disobey the commands set down, He said:

> *"My Spirit shall not strive with man forever,*
> *for he is indeed flesh."*
>
> Genesis 6:3a

About two thousand years would pass from when these words were prophesied to their fulfilment when Zechariah was killed for proclaiming the word of the Lord which said:

> *"Why do you transgress*
> *the commandments of the Lord,*
> *so that you cannot prosper?*
> *Because you have forsaken the Lord,*
> *He also has forsaken you."*
>
> 2 Chronicles 24:20

After this act of murder against the Lord's servant, four hundred years passed before the Lord revealed Himself to another prophet by the name of Zacharias, who was completing his duties in the temple on Yon Kippur, the most holy day of the year.

John the Baptist paved the way for the third blessing to be fulfilled as he was the forerunner to the Saviour of the world. But as with the past, the people of Israel grumbled with the answer the Lord had supplied for their future. Hindsight demonstrates that the Israelites were never satisfied with the things the Lord provided, as they didn't trust the Lord and wanted things done their way. From when Moses talked with the leaders, the plagues, the Egyptian army at the Red Sea, through the supply of their need in manna and quail, these people always grumbled.

When Moses and Joshua didn't return in their expected timeframe, the Israelites sought an alternative god, the golden calf. When Pilate offered Jesus as the *'King of the Jews'* to the people, they chose the alternative, Barabbas. All these years later, the Lord's plan for His people is once more rejected as what the Lord ordained did not suit their expectations. Peter would at a later stage confront the Jews with their act of murder against God's anointed Son when he said:

> *"Jesus, being delivered by the determined purpose*
> *and foreknowledge of God,*
> *you have taken by lawless hands,*

> *have crucified, and put to death;*
> *whom God raised up,*
> *having loosed the pains of death,*
> *because it was not possible*
> *that He should be held by it."*
>
> Acts 2:23–24

This act by the rulers of the Jews released the prophesy of Simeon when he looked at the baby Jesus in his arms and said:

> *"For my eyes have seen Your salvation*
> *which You have prepared before the face of all peoples,*
> *a light to bring revelation to the Gentiles,*
> *and the glory of Your people Israel."*
>
> Luke 2:30–32

The third blessing given to Abram said:

> *"I will bless those who bless you,*
> *and I will curse him who curses you;*
> *and in you all the families of the earth*
> *shall be blessed."*
>
> Genesis 12:3

Paul when writing to the Galatians explained that when the rulers of the Jews refused and denied the supremacy of Christ, the way was now opened for the Gentiles to be grafted into the Body of Christ.

> *"Christ has redeemed us from the curse of the law,*
> *having become a curse for us,*
> *that the blessing of Abraham*
> *might come upon the Gentiles in Jesus Christ,*
> *that we might receive the promise*
> *of the Spirit through faith."*
>
> Galatians 3:14

About four thousand years had passed from the bloodline of Adam to the ministry of Jesus. Approximately, one thousand eight hundred years had elapsed from the covenant with Abram to the death and resurrection of Jesus Christ, the Messiah, to bring into place the third blessing that would allow the Holy Spirit to be released, so that not only fellowship with the Father was regained, but the power to live a life that was pleasing to Father God was possible.

Under the Law, fellowship and power were unobtainable by completed works, but by the Grace of God, we are enabled to walk right into the presence of God the Father, through Jesus' resurrection. The sacrificial life that Jesus lived here on earth, coupled with the faith we are all given, make us righteous in the sight of Father God. We are right with God, as the blood of Jesus covers our shortcomings and sin because we have fallen from right standing, but through true repentance, we are cleansed for all sin and are seen by the Father as clean.

Only those who have been chosen, experience the three blessings, as there is nothing we can do to gain what the Lord will give freely to His choice people, as He said, *"For many are called, but few are choice"* (Matthew 22:14). When the Apostle John, the earthly cousin of Jesus wrote the *'Book of the Revelation'*, outlined in no uncertain terms, who would fellowship with Him in the last days for Jesus said:

> *"Behold, I stand at the door and knock.*
> *If anyone hears My voice and opens the door,*
> *I will come to him and dine with him,*
> *and he with Me."*
>
> Revelation 3:20

The children of Israel were given the choice to obey the command of the Lord, go into the promised land and possess what Father God had provided for them, but they disobeyed and those over twenty years of age, perished in the desert. Joshua and Caleb and those under twenty were allowed to accept the blessing the Lord had foretold.

The Jewish people were also given the opportunity to possess the promised land, but because they chose Barabbas instead of

Jesus, the outcome for the majority was foretold by Jesus when He said:

"Therefore I said to you

that you will die in your sins;

for if you do not believe that I am He,

you will die in your sins."

John 8:24

Only a small remnant believed in Jesus, so the words Jesus proclaimed applied to the rest of the Jewish race and they would perish just like their ancestors did. Because the Jews were living under the law, just as the sin of Nathan (Joshua 7:10–25) affected all the children of Israel, the ruling of the minority religious leaders applied to those who did not accept Jesus as Lord and Saviour.

The Holy Spirit is alive and active in our present world, as He calls those who would accept the promised blessings and eternity in the presence of the Father, the Son and the Holy Spirit. The offer is not one of our choosing because:

"You did not choose Me,

but I chose you and appointed you

that you should go and bear fruit,

and that your fruit should remain,

> *that whatever you ask the Father*
> *in My name He may give you."*

John 15:16

Jesus is still pleading with those He would choose to be part of *'the called'* as He stands at the door of your heart and knocks. The way to eternal life can be only found in Jesus, as this is what you are offered. As you have free will, it is your choice to accept or reject His offer to you.

The door to the Promised Land is opened to you but will not always remain open. The three promises are offered to each person, a land of their own which is Beulah Land or the place Jesus has gone to prepare for each of His followers. A mighty nation is the kingdom of priests who worship Father God and remain in His presence for eternity. A blessing to others will occur when we are one mind in Jesus, as nothing will inhibit all those in fellowship with the Creator. Paul when writing his second letter to the Corinthians used some words written by Isaiah.

> *"In an acceptable time*
> *I have heard you,*
> *and in the day of Salvation*
> *I have helped you."*

Isaiah 49:8

The Lord made a covenant with the earth that *"While the earth remains, seedtime and harvest, cold and heat, winter and summer, and day and night shall not cease"* (Genesis 8:22). There is a time when the earth will not remain and this covenant will conclude, just as the accepted time to accept the Lord and His salvation. Jesus will fulfil the three promises given to Abraham when He returns, and we know this is true, as God is a promise keeper, He cannot lie, and His word does not change.

We do not know when His return will occur, we just need to be ready as we are told His return will be in the twinkling of an eye (1 Corinthians 15:52), as a flash of lightning (Matthew 24:27), and as a thief in the night (1 Thessalonians 5:2). The psalmist wrote words to describe the return of Jesus when they said:

> *"The nations raged,*
> *the kingdoms were moved;*
> *He uttered His voice, the earth melted."*
>
> Psalm 46:6

Jesus added further teaching about His return when He shared the following privately with Peter, James, John, and Andrew as they sat on the Mount of Olives about the signs of the times and the end of the age.

> *"But in those days, after that the tribulation,*
> *the sun will be darkened,*

and the moon will not give its light;
the stars of heaven will fall,
and the powers in the heavens will be shaken.
Then they will see the Son of Man coming
in the clouds with great power and glory.
And then He will send His angels,
and gather together His elect
from the four winds,
from the farthest part of earth
to the farthest part of heaven."

Mark 13:24–27

A Benediction

Rev Ernest William Blandly was a man in some respects like Moses. He was born in the United Kingdom, in 1848 and became a British minister, then migrated to the USA in 1884 where he became an officer in The Salvation Army. Some forty years had passed when he had a calling to live in a Manhattan New York slum called "Hell's Kitchen" with gangs and low life which became a reality in 1890. As Moses led the children out of captivity, so Rev Blandly led many a lost soul out of the slums and into the light of heaven.

A text that marked his life was:

> *"Whoever desires to come after Me,*
> *let him deny himself,*
> *and take up his cross,*
> *and follow Me."*
>
> Mark 8:34

Rev Blandly wrote the following song that reflected his life and ministry.

The Path of Life

I can hear my Saviour calling,
I can hear my Saviour calling,
I can hear my Saviour calling,
'Take thy cross and follow, follow Me'.

Refrain:
Where He leads me I will follow,
Where He leads me I will follow,
Where He leads me I will follow,
I'll go with Him, with Him all the way.

I'll go with Him through the garden,
I'll go with Him through the garden,
I'll go with Him through the garden,
I'll go with Him, with Him all the way. *[Refrain]*

I'll go with Him through the judgment,
I'll go with Him through the judgment,
I'll go with Him through the judgment,
I'll go with Him, with Him all the way. *[Refrain]*

He will give me grace and glory,
He will give me grace and glory,
He will give me grace and glory,
And go with me, with me all the way. *[Refrain]*

Public Domain

Other Books by the Author
Available from www.wittonbooks.com

Betrayal can be found anywhere. It is not confined to two people. Family, friends, work colleagues, recreational groups, and the church. Betrayal manifests itself wherever two or three are gathered.

Seven characters from the Old Testament are featured to show 'Betrayal' as the force that cost them their life or made them spiritually stronger.

Abel, Noah, Job, Joseph, Gideon, Samson, David, Jesus, and Judas are included.

As each of their lives is studied, in the main, one thing that never suffered defeat was their love for Father God. In return, He provided all they needed including protection from the evil forces. Judas was the exception.

After attending a pre-Christmas church eveing, I came away feeling numb due to the presentation of the Christmas story, by very secular people.

As you read, my prayer is that the Holy spirit will not only impart wisdom, but a deep understanding of the real Nativity story.

Available from www.wittonbooks.com

Have you ever searched the four gospels to obtain the full account of Jesus' life?

The author, under the guidance of the Holy Spirit, took the words of the Apostle Paul to heart, when the latter wrote to Timothy and encouraged him to "Study to show yourself approved unto God, a workman that needs not be ashamed, rightly dividing the word of truth."

2 Timothy 2:15

In *The Life of Jesus: A Simple Narrative* the author uses language similar to the New King James Version of the Bible to order and blend the four gospels into one complete story.

In the second book, *The Life of Christ Simply Told*, the author uses language similar to the New International Version of the Bible to order and blend the four gospels into the complete story of Jesus' life.

Available from www.wittonbooks.com

God, Man, Lucifer and the End Time contains a collection of seven stand-alone documents. However, they all overlap and combine in a way only the Holy Spirit could implement. They are complex topics, requiring a great deal of study to 'bring it together'.

Prompted by the Holy Spirit and this work used as the 'foundation', may it lead to a greater understanding of the truth, majesty and love of our God.

Life's a Journey introduces the reader to the roads taken by several Bible characters and the consequences of their chosen walks. Those introduced are Mary, John the Baptist, Andrew, John the Disciple, and the children of Israel.

A second section brings a light-hearted twist, as the author shares real-life incidents, although the setting has been changed to add further humour to the already hilarious accounts of his eventful life.

Each of us has a journey to walk. Some long, some short, and some heart-breaking, others blessed. May each who reads glean encouragement for your life's walk.

Available from www.wittonbooks.com
and *The Adventures of Max* Facebook page

Series titles available:

Book 1	*The Defiant Mouse*
Book 2	*The Curious Chicken*
Book 3	*A Dog in Need*
Book 4	*An Old Friend Found*
Book 5	*The Rescue*
Book 6	*The Bush Fire*
Book 7	*A Bad Influence*
Book 8	*A Shining Light*
Book 9	*Hidden Secrets*
Book 10	*A Foiled Plot*
Book 11	*Running the Race*
Book 12	*An Unexpected Reward*
Book 13	*Max Meets a Friend*
Book 14	*Reflections*

**Available from www.wittonbooks.com
and *Manuel's Missions* Facebook page**

Series titles available:

Book 1	*The Servant Mouse*
Book 2	*A Cherished Place*
Book 3	*Manuel and the Spider*
Book 4	*A Generous Giver*
Book 5	*Lost and Found*
Book 6	*Manuel's Day Out*
Book 7	*Love One Another*
Book 8	*Observations*

www.ingramcontent.com/pod-product-compliance
Lightning Source LLC
Chambersburg PA
CBHW051424290426
44109CB00016B/1429